EMBRACING GRIEF: NAVIGATING LOSS WITH COURAGE AND RESILIENCE

NICOLE J BARKER

TABLE OF CONTENT

Disclaimer

The names mentioned in the stories shared here are fictitious and are intended to protect the privacy and confidentiality of the individuals involved. While the experiences and narratives presented may be inspired by real-life situations encountered in therapeutic settings, they have been fictionalized to ensure anonymity.

It's important to note that the individuals portrayed in these stories have willingly shared their experiences for the purpose of providing support, understanding, and comfort to others who may be navigating similar challenges. Their stories are offered with the intention of fostering empathy, connection, and solidarity among those who are grieving or facing difficult times.

By sharing these stories, it is our hope to create a space where individuals can feel validated, understood, and supported in their own journeys of grief and healing. It is also a reminder that grief is a natural and universal experience, and that seeking support and connection during times of loss is not only acceptable but encouraged.

However, it's important to remember that each person's grief journey is unique, and what works for one individual may not necessarily work for another. Therefore, while these stories may offer insights and perspectives, they should not be considered as a substitute for professional advice or guidance. If you are struggling with grief or any other emotional difficulties, we encourage you to reach out to a qualified mental health professional for personalized support and assistance.

Above all, please know that you are not alone in your journey, and it's okay to seek help and support when needed. Grieving is a natural and essential part of the human experience, and by sharing our stories and supporting one another, we can find solace, strength, and healing together.

Dedication

To those who have experienced the profound pain of loss and the journey of grief, this book is dedicated to you. Your resilience, courage, and capacity for love inspire us all. May these words offer solace, guidance, and a beacon of hope as you navigate the complex emotions of loss and find your path toward healing. You are not alone.

Preface

In writing this book, I embarked on a journey that led me to the heart of one of life's most profound experiences: death and grief. It is a journey that began with my own encounters with loss, where I grappled with the overwhelming waves of sorrow and sought understanding amidst the chaos of emotions.

Through my personal experiences and the stories of countless others, I have come to realize the universality of grief – a journey that transcends age, gender, culture, and beliefs. It is a journey marked by pain, confusion, and profound transformation.

In these pages, I offer not just words, but a companion for those who find themselves navigating the complex terrain of grief. Drawing from the wisdom of experts, the resilience of survivors, and the depths of my own soul, I aim to illuminate the path toward healing and hope.

This book is not a prescription for grief, nor is it a roadmap with all the answers. Instead, it is an invitation – an invitation to embrace the full spectrum of emotions, to honor the memories of those we have lost, and to find solace in the shared humanity that binds us all.

As you embark on this journey with me, may you find comfort in knowing that you are not alone. May these pages serve as a gentle reminder that even in the darkest of moments, there is light to be found, and healing to be embraced.

With heartfelt sincerity,

Nicole J Barker

Introduction

In the quiet moments of the night, when the weight of your grief feels unbearable and the ache in your heart seems never-ending, you may find yourself searching for answers. You may wonder how you will ever find the strength to navigate the turbulent waters of grief, to make sense of the profound loss that has shattered your world.

In these moments, know that you are not alone. This book is written for you – the one who has known the depths of sorrow, the one who has felt the sting of death's embrace. It is an offering of solace, a beacon of light in the darkness, and a gentle reminder that amidst the pain, there is hope.

Throughout these pages, we will embark on a journey together – a journey of healing, understanding, and transformation. We will explore the complexities of grief, the intricacies of loss, and the resilience of the human spirit. And as we navigate this terrain, my hope is that you will find comfort, clarity, and a sense of companionship along the way.

Though the road ahead may be long and winding, remember that every step you take is a testament to your strength and courage. You have the power within you to not only survive, but to thrive in the face of adversity. And as we embark on this journey together, know that I am here to walk beside you, offering support, empathy, and unwavering compassion.

So, let us begin. Let us honor the memories of those we have lost, celebrate the love that binds us together, and embrace the journey of healing that lies ahead. For in the depths of grief, there is also the promise of renewal, the possibility of growth, and the enduring beauty of the human spirit.

Welcome to a journey of healing, hope, and profound transformation. Welcome to this sacred space of understanding and compassion. Welcome home.

Chapter 1: Understanding Grief

Grief is not simply an emotion; it is a profound and different experience that encompasses a wide range of emotions, thoughts, and behaviors. It is a natural response to loss, whether that loss is the death of a loved one, the end of a relationship, or any significant change or upheaval in one's life.

At its core, grief is a deeply personal journey, unique to each individual who experiences it. No two people grieve in exactly the same way, and there is no right or wrong way to grieve. It is a process that unfolds in its own time and in its own way, guided by the unique circumstances of the loss and the individual's own coping mechanisms and support systems.

One of the most common misconceptions about grief is that it follows a linear path, with a clear beginning, middle, and end. In reality, grief is more like a winding road, full of twists and turns, ups and downs. It is marked by moments of intense pain and sorrow, as well as moments of calm and acceptance. And just when you think you have reached the end of the road, you may find yourself revisiting earlier stages of grief, cycling through the process once again.

The journey of grief is often characterized by a series of stages or phases, first proposed by psychiatrist Elisabeth Kübler-Ross in her groundbreaking book "On Death and Dying." These stages – denial, anger, bargaining, depression, and acceptance – are not meant to be rigid or prescriptive, but rather serve as a framework for understanding the range of emotions that individuals may experience as they process their grief.

In addition to these stages, grief can also manifest in a variety of physical, emotional, and psychological ways. Physical symptoms such as fatigue, insomnia, and loss of appetite are common, as are emotional symptoms like sadness, guilt, and anxiety. It is not uncommon for individuals experiencing grief to also grapple with feelings of numbness, confusion, or even anger at themselves, others, or the world around them.

When we experience loss, whether it be the death of a loved one, the end of a relationship, or the loss of a dream, we are thrust into a world of uncertainty and pain. Grief washes over us like a tidal wave, engulfing us in a sea of emotions – sadness, anger, guilt, confusion, and despair.

But grief is not just about the emotions we feel; it is also about the thoughts that consume us and the behaviors that define us. It is about the questions we ask ourselves – Why did this happen? What could I have done differently? How will I ever go on without them? – and the endless search for meaning and understanding in the face of tragedy.

And when we experience loss, whether through death, separation, or the dissolution of a dream, we are thrust into the depths of grief's abyss. It is a place of darkness and despair, where the pain of our sorrow threatens to overwhelm us. Yet, amidst the shadows, there is also the glimmer of light – a beacon of hope that guides us through the darkest of nights.

Grief is a complex amalgamation of emotions, thoughts, and sensations. It is the raw ache of longing, the searing pain of absence, and the silent scream of anguish that echoes in the depths of our souls. It is the silent tears that fall when no one is watching, the bittersweet memories that haunt our dreams, and the relentless ache of yearning for what once was.

But grief is not just about the pain we feel; it is also about the growth that emerges from our suffering. It is a journey of self-discovery and transformation, as we navigate the labyrinth of our emotions and emerge on the other side, stronger, wiser, and more compassionate than before. It is through our experiences of loss that we come to understand the true value of life and the preciousness of every moment we are given.

One of the most profound aspects of grief is its universality. No one is immune to its touch, and no one escapes its grasp unscathed. It is a shared experience that binds us together in our common humanity, bridging the gaps that separate us and forging connections that transcend time and space.

In our society, grief is often seen as something to be endured, a burden to be borne in silence. But the truth is that grief is a natural and necessary part of the human experience. It is the price we pay for love, the flip side of the coin that reminds us of the depth of our connections and the fragility of life.

Furthermore, grief is a journey that transcends time, space, and understanding. It is a deeply personal experience that defies explanation, yet binds us together in our shared humanity. At its core, grief is a testament to the depth of our love and the profound impact that loss has on our lives.

As we journey through grief, it is important to remember that healing is not a linear process, but a winding path with many twists and turns. It is a journey of peaks and valleys, of highs and lows, as we navigate the ever-changing landscape of our emotions. And though the road may be long and arduous, know that you are not alone. There is comfort in the knowledge that others have walked this path before you, and that there is hope on the horizon, waiting to greet you with open arms.

In the pages that follow, we will explore why it affect us so deeply, and its potential for transformation. We will delve into the depths of sorrow and emerge with a newfound sense of resilience and strength. And though the journey may be difficult, know that you have within you the power to overcome, to heal, and to find peace amidst the storm.

- What is grief and why does it affect us so deeply?

Grief is a profound and complex emotional response to loss. It encompasses a wide range of feelings, thoughts, and behaviors that individuals experience when they are faced with the death of a loved one, the end of a relationship, or any significant change or loss in their lives.

At its core, grief is a natural and universal human experience. One reason why grief affects us so deeply is its inherent unpredictability. Unlike other emotions that may ebb and flow with relative predictability, grief has a way of sneaking up on us when we least expect it. It can ambush us in the midst of everyday activities, triggered by a fleeting memory, a familiar scent, or a passing thought. This unpredictability can leave us feeling as though we are navigating a minefield of emotions, never knowing when the next wave of grief will hit.

It also affects us deeply because it strikes at the very heart of our sense of identity, belonging, and connection. When we experience loss, we are confronted with the reality of our own mortality and the impermanence of life. This can evoke a myriad of emotions, including sadness, anger, guilt, confusion, and despair.

Additionally, grief affects us deeply because it disrupts our sense of time and space. In the throes of grief, the past, present, and future blur together in a maelstrom of memories, regrets, and what-ifs. We may find ourselves dwelling on the past, replaying moments with our loved ones over and over again in a futile attempt to hold onto what has been lost. Or we may find ourselves consumed by anxiety about the future, grappling with fears about what lies ahead in a world that feels infinitely changed.

Grief also affects us deeply because it challenges our sense of control and security. Loss disrupts the familiar patterns and routines of our lives, leaving us feeling adrift and vulnerable. It can shake our beliefs and assumptions about the world, forcing us to confront uncomfortable truths and grapple with existential questions about the meaning and purpose of life.

Furthermore, grief is a deeply personal and individual experience. Each person's experience of grief is unique, shaped by their personality, background, beliefs, and relationship to the person or thing they have lost. This can make grief feel isolating and overwhelming, as individuals struggle to make sense of their emotions and find ways to cope with their loss.

Moreover, grief affects us deeply because it demands that we confront our deepest fears and vulnerabilities. In the face of loss, we are forced to confront our mortality, the impermanence of life, and the inevitability of change. This confrontation can trigger a profound existential crisis, prompting us to reevaluate our beliefs, values, and priorities in light of our newfound understanding of life's fragility.

Additionally, grief affects us deeply because it challenges our sense of identity and self-concept. The loss of a loved one, a relationship, or a cherished dream can leave us feeling as though a part of ourselves has been lost along with them. We may grapple with feelings of emptiness, confusion, and a profound sense of longing as we struggle to come to terms with the void left in their absence.

Similarly , grief affects us deeply because it challenges our sense of self and identity. In the wake of loss, we may find ourselves struggling to make sense of who we are in the absence of the person or thing we have lost. We may question our beliefs, values, and priorities, as we grapple with the profound existential questions that loss inevitably raises.

Furthermore, grief affects us deeply because it disrupts our social networks and support systems. The loss of a loved one can leave us feeling isolated and alone, as we navigate the complex terrain of grief without the presence of those who once provided us with comfort, companionship, and understanding.

In addition , grief affects us deeply because it challenges our sense of control and agency. In the face of loss, we may find ourselves grappling with feelings of powerlessness and helplessness, as we come to terms with the reality that some things in life are simply beyond our control. This loss of control can be profoundly unsettling, leaving us feeling vulnerable and exposed in a world that suddenly feels uncertain and unpredictable.

And lastly , grief affects us deeply because it forces us to confront our own mortality. In the face of loss, we are confronted with the stark reality of death – a reality that can be difficult to accept and even harder to comprehend. This confrontation with mortality can evoke a profound sense of existential angst, as we grapple with the uncertainty of what lies beyond and the ultimate meaning of our existence.

Ultimately, grief affects us deeply because it touches every aspect of our being – our emotions, thoughts, physical sensations, and behaviors. It challenges us to confront the reality of loss and to find ways to integrate that loss into our lives in a way that honors our memories and allows us to move forward with hope and resilience.

- The emotional , physical and psychological processes of grief

The process of grief is a deeply personal and individual journey that unfolds in its own time and in its own way for each person. While there is no one-size-fits-all approach to grieving, there are common patterns and stages that many people may experience as they navigate their way through grief.

The emotional, physical, and psychological processes of grief intertwine in a complex and different dance, each aspect influencing and shaping the others in profound ways.

Emotionally, grief manifests as a kaleidoscope of feelings that can range from profound sadness and despair to anger, guilt, and even relief. These emotions may come in waves, washing over us with intensity or lingering quietly beneath the surface, waiting to be acknowledged and expressed. At times, the emotional pain of grief may feel unbearable, leaving us feeling overwhelmed and consumed by our sorrow. Other times, it may feel like a dull ache, a constant reminder of the void left by our loss.

Physically, grief can take a toll on our bodies in a variety of ways. It may manifest as physical symptoms such as fatigue, insomnia, headaches, muscle tension, and changes in appetite or weight. These physical symptoms are often the body's way of expressing the stress and strain of grief, as well as the toll that emotional pain can take on our physical well-being. Additionally, grief can weaken the immune system, making us more susceptible to illness and disease.

Psychologically, grief can have a profound impact on our thoughts, beliefs, and perceptions of the world around us. It may lead to feelings of confusion, disorientation, and a sense of unreality as we struggle to come to terms with the enormity of our loss. It may also trigger existential questions about the meaning and purpose of life, as we grapple with the uncertainty of what lies beyond and the ultimate significance of our existence. Additionally, grief can affect our cognitive functioning, making it difficult to concentrate, remember things, or make decisions.

Let's breakdown these processes:

A.Emotional Processes:

I.   Sadness: This is the most prominent emotion associated with grief and can manifest as deep sorrow, longing, and loneliness.

II. Anger: Anger can be directed towards the deceased, oneself, or even the situation. It stems from feelings of unfairness, frustration, and helplessness.

III. Guilt: Individuals may experience survivor's guilt, questioning their actions or feeling responsible for the loss.

IV. Fear: The uncertainty of the future and the fear of additional losses can be a significant source of anxiety and fear

V.   Denial: As a coping mechanism, individuals might deny the reality of the loss, delaying or mitigating the initial emotional impact.

VI. Isolation: Withdrawing from social interactions and isolating oneself can be a temporary response to cope with the overwhelming emotions.

B. Physical Processes:

I. Changes in sleep patterns: Difficulty sleeping, insomnia, or excessive sleepiness are common.

II. Changes in appetite: Loss of appetite or emotional eating can occur due to stress and emotional turmoil.

III. Fatigue and weakness: The emotional strain can lead to physical exhaustion and a lack of energy.

IV. Physical aches and pains: Headaches, muscle tension, and stomach problems can manifest due to the stress response.

V. Weakened immune system: Grief can compromise the immune system, making individuals more susceptible to illness.

C. Psychological Processes:

I. Loss of meaning and purpose: The loss can disrupt one's sense of purpose and meaning in life, leading to existential questioning.
II. Difficulty concentrating: The emotional state can affect cognitive function, making it challenging to focus or complete tasks.
III. Flashbacks and intrusive thoughts: Vivid memories or unwanted thoughts about the loss can be intrusive and disruptive.
IV. Changes in identity: Losing someone close can alter one's sense of self and identity, especially if the deceased played a significant role in their life.
V. Post-traumatic stress disorder (PTSD): In some cases, individuals may experience symptoms of PTSD if the loss involved a traumatic experience.

It's important to remember that these processes are not linear, and individuals may experience them in varying degrees and at different times throughout their grief journey. Seeking professional support from therapists specializing in grief can be beneficial in navigating these complex processes and finding healthy ways to cope with the loss.

Together, these emotional, physical, and psychological processes create a complex pattern of grief that is as unique and individual as the person experiencing it. Understanding and navigating these processes is an essential part of the grieving journey.

- Realizing that grief is a natural part of life and love

Realizing that grief is a natural part of life and love is a profound and transformative realization that can shift our perspective on loss and suffering.

Grief is not a sign of weakness , but rather a testament to the depth of our love and the significance of what we have lost. It is a natural and inevitable part of the human experience, woven into the fabric of our lives and inseparable from the bonds of love and connection that unite us.

When we come to understand that grief is a natural part of life and love, we are able to embrace our pain and sorrow with greater acceptance and compassion. We no longer see grief as something to be avoided or suppressed, but rather as a sacred and necessary part of the healing process.

Realizing that grief is a natural part of life and love also allows us to approach our experiences of loss with greater resilience and strength. Instead of being overwhelmed by our grief, we can find solace in the knowledge that our pain is a testament to the depth of our love and the significance of what we have lost.

Furthermore, realizing that grief is a natural part of life and love can inspire us to cherish the moments we have with our loved ones more deeply and to cultivate greater gratitude and appreciation for the preciousness of life. It reminds us to savor the simple joys and fleeting moments of connection that make life worth living, knowing that one day they may be gone.

It allows us to recognize that grief is not a sign of failure, but rather a testament to the depth of our connections and the richness of our human experience. It is a natural response to the inevitable changes and transitions that shape our lives, and a reminder of the preciousness of the moments we share with our loved ones.

When we come to understand that grief is a natural part of life and love, we are freed from the burden of shame and guilt that often accompanies our pain. Instead of viewing grief as something to be endured in silence, we can embrace it as a vital aspect of the human condition – a sacred and necessary part of the healing process.

Moreover, realizing that grief is a natural part of life and love empowers us to navigate our experiences of loss with greater resilience and grace. It reminds us that we are not alone in our suffering, but part of a larger community of individuals who have experienced similar pain and sorrow. This sense of connection can provide comfort and support as we journey through the depths of our grief.

Furthermore, realizing that grief is a natural part of life and love can inspire us to live more fully and authentically in the present moment. It encourages us to cherish the relationships and experiences that bring meaning and joy to our lives, knowing that they are fleeting and precious.

Realizing that grief is a natural part of life and love also invites us to approach our experiences of loss with a greater sense of curiosity and openness. Instead of viewing grief as something to be feared or avoided, we can see it as an opportunity for growth and transformation.

When we embrace the inevitability of grief, we give ourselves permission to explore the depths of our emotions with curiosity and compassion. We allow ourselves to sit with our pain and sorrow, to acknowledge and honor our feelings without judgment or resistance. In doing so, we create space for healing and self-discovery, uncovering hidden strengths and resilience we may not have known we possessed.

Moreover, realizing that grief is a natural part of life and love encourages us to cultivate a deeper sense of empathy and compassion for ourselves and others. It reminds us that we are all vulnerable to loss and suffering, and that our experiences of grief connect us in profound and meaningful ways. By embracing our own grief with compassion, we can extend that same compassion to others who are struggling with their own losses.

Furthermore, realizing that grief is a natural part of life and love empowers us to find meaning and purpose in the midst of our suffering. It encourages us to seek out sources of support and connection, whether through therapy, support groups, or simply reaching out to friends and loved ones. It reminds us that even in our darkest moments, there is hope, and that healing is possible with time, patience, and self-care.

Ultimately, realizing that grief is a natural part of life and love invites us to embrace the fullness of our human experience – the joy and the sorrow, the love and the loss. It is a reminder that even in our moments of deepest despair, we are not alone, and that there is beauty to be found in the midst of our pain.

Chapter 2: Coping Strategies and Tools

Coping strategies and tools are essential resources that can help individuals navigate the challenging terrain of grief and find healing and resilience in the face of loss. While the journey of grief is deeply personal and unique to each individual, there are a variety of strategies and tools that can provide support and comfort along the way.

1. Seeking Support: One of the most important coping strategies for grief is reaching out for support from friends, family, or a professional counselor. Talking openly about your feelings and experiences can provide validation and comfort, and help you feel less alone in your grief.

2. Self-Care: Taking care of your physical, emotional, and spiritual well-being is essential during times of grief. This may include getting enough rest, eating nutritious foods, engaging in

regular exercise, practicing relaxation techniques such as deep breathing or meditation, and finding activities that bring you joy and comfort.

3. Expressing Emotions: Allowing yourself to feel and express your emotions in healthy ways can be an important part of the grieving process. This may include journaling, creating art, participating in support groups, or engaging in rituals or ceremonies that honor your loved one's memory.

4. Setting Boundaries: Recognize your limits and give yourself permission to set boundaries with others as needed. This may mean taking time for yourself when you need it, saying no to activities or obligations that feel overwhelming, or limiting exposure to people or situations that are triggering or unhelpful.

5. Finding Meaning: Searching for meaning and purpose in the midst of grief can be a powerful coping strategy. This may involve finding ways to honor your loved one's memory, connecting with your spiritual or religious beliefs, or

seeking out opportunities for personal growth and transformation.

6. Creating Rituals: Rituals and traditions can provide structure and comfort during times of grief. Whether it's lighting a candle, visiting a special place, or holding a memorial service, rituals can help you feel connected to your loved one and provide a sense of continuity and meaning.

7. Seeking Professional Help: If you're struggling to cope with your grief or experiencing symptoms of depression or anxiety, don't hesitate to seek help from a qualified mental health professional. Therapy, counseling, or support groups can provide additional support and guidance as you navigate your grief journey.

Remember, coping with grief is a gradual process that takes time and patience. Be gentle with yourself and allow yourself to grieve in your own way and at your own pace. With the support of others and the use of coping strategies and tools, you can find healing and resilience in the midst of loss.

- Practical strategies for coping with loss

Practical strategies are crucial for managing the difficulties of grief in day-to-day existence. In the middle of their loss, people can find stability and comfort in these solutions, which offer concrete skills and actions to control emotions and preserve wellbeing.

1. Manage your immediate needs:

I. Create a routine: Having a schedule can provide structure and a sense of normalcy during this challenging time. Maintain regular sleep patterns, eat healthy meals, and get some exercise.

II. Delegate and ask for help: Don't hesitate to reach out to friends, family, or even professional services for help with errands, household chores, or childcare.

Accepting support can reduce stress and give you space to grieve.

III. Take care of legal and financial matters: Deal with any immediate legal or financial tasks related to the loss, such as notifying relevant institutions, attending to necessary paperwork, and seeking legal advice if needed.

2. Manage your emotions:

I. Practice mindfulness and relaxation techniques: Techniques like deep breathing, meditation, yoga, or spending time in nature can help manage stress and anxiety associated with grief.

II. Engage in creative expression: Journaling, writing poems, creating art, or playing music can be a healthy way to express your emotions and find solace.

III. Connect with others in a safe space: Talking about your feelings with trusted friends, family, or a therapist can be incredibly helpful in processing your emotions and finding support. Consider joining a support group to connect with others who understand your experience.

3. Create space for remembrance and rituals:

I. Create rituals or traditions: This could include visiting a special place, lighting a candle, sharing stories about the deceased, or engaging in activities they enjoyed. Rituals can provide comfort and a sense of connection.

II. Practice self-care rituals: Prioritize activities that bring you comfort and relaxation, like taking a warm bath, reading a book, or spending time in nature. Taking care of yourself is crucial during this time.

III. Maintain connections with the deceased (if comfortable): Some individuals find comfort in keeping the deceased's memory alive by looking at photos, listening to their favorite music, or keeping their belongings close. Choose what feels right for you.

4. Remember, there's no right or wrong way to grieve:

I. Be patient with yourself: Everyone grieves differently and at their own pace. Don't compare your journey to others. Allow yourself to feel the full range of emotions associated with the loss.

II. Be kind to yourself: Avoid harsh self-criticism or judgment. This is a difficult time, and it's important to practice self-compassion and understanding.

III. Seek professional help if needed: If you're struggling to cope with the loss, don't hesitate to seek professional support from a therapist or counselor who specializes in grief.

Additional Tips:

I. Limit alcohol and drugs: These substances may offer temporary relief but can hinder the healing process and exacerbate emotional distress.

II. Maintain healthy habits: Ensure you're getting enough sleep, eating nutritious food, and exercising regularly. These practices can improve your overall well-being and emotional resilience.

III. Be patient with those around you: People who care about you may not know how to best support you during this time. Be patient and communicate your needs clearly.

Remember, coping with loss is a gradual process. While these strategies can provide practical tools, be patient and compassionate with yourself. Allow yourself to grieve and seek support when needed.

- Insights on how to navigate the grieving process with resilience

Navigating the grieving process with resilience requires a different approach that encompasses self-awareness, self-care, and support from others. It's a deeply personal journey, unique to each individual, but there are universal insights that can help guide you through this challenging time.

First and foremost, it's crucial to acknowledge and accept your feelings. Grief is a complex and unpredictable emotion, and it's normal to experience a wide range of feelings such as sadness, anger, guilt, and even relief. Rather than pushing these feelings away or judging yourself for having them, try to approach them with compassion and curiosity. Allow yourself to sit with your emotions, explore them, and express them in healthy ways.

Seeking support is another key aspect of navigating grief with resilience. It's important to reach out to friends, family members, or a therapist who can offer a listening ear, practical assistance, and emotional support. Talking openly about your feelings and experiences can provide validation and comfort, and help you feel less isolated in your grief. Remember, you don't have to go through this alone.

Taking care of yourself is essential during the grieving process. This means attending to your physical, emotional, and spiritual well-being. Make sure to get enough rest, eat nutritious foods, engage in regular exercise, and practice relaxation techniques such as deep breathing or meditation. Taking care of yourself can help you manage stress, maintain your resilience, and cope more effectively with your grief.

Setting boundaries is also important as you navigate the grieving process. Recognize your limits and give yourself permission to set boundaries with others as needed. This may involve taking breaks from social interactions or activities that feel overwhelming, or setting boundaries around topics of conversation that are triggering or unhelpful. Remember, it's okay to prioritize your own well-being and needs.

Finding meaning in your grief journey can provide a sense of purpose and direction as you navigate through the pain and sorrow. This may involve honoring your loved one's memory through rituals or traditions, finding opportunities for personal growth and transformation, or seeking out ways to make a positive impact in the world in their honor. Finding meaning can help you find hope and resilience in the midst of your loss.

In addition to the aforementioned strategies, it's important to recognize that grief can often bring up unexpected challenges and triggers. As you navigate the grieving process with resilience, it's helpful to anticipate potential difficulties and develop strategies for coping with them.

One way to cope with unexpected challenges is to practice mindfulness and present moment awareness. Mindfulness involves bringing your attention to the present moment without judgment, allowing you to observe your thoughts, feelings, and sensations with compassion and acceptance. By staying grounded in the present moment, you can reduce the impact of intrusive thoughts or overwhelming emotions, and respond to challenges with greater clarity and equanimity.

Another helpful strategy is to cultivate a sense of gratitude and appreciation for the moments of joy and connection that still exist in your life, even amidst the pain of grief. Taking time each day to reflect on the things you are grateful for can help shift your focus away from your loss and towards the positive aspects of your life. This can provide a sense of perspective and resilience, helping you find moments of lightness and hope in the midst of darkness.

Additionally, consider incorporating creative expression into your grieving process as a way of processing your emotions and honoring your loved one's memory. Whether it's writing, painting, music, or another form of artistic expression, creative outlets can provide a cathartic release for your feelings and allow you to channel your grief into something meaningful and transformative.

Another important aspect of coping with grief is finding ways to honor and remember your loved one who has passed away. This can be a meaningful way to keep their memory alive and maintain a sense of connection with them, even after they're gone.

One way to honor your loved one is by creating a memorial or tribute in their honor. This could involve planting a tree or garden in their memory, creating a scrapbook or photo album of cherished memories, or dedicating a special place or object to them. By creating a tangible reminder of your loved one, you can keep their memory alive and find comfort in knowing that they will always be with you in spirit.

Another way to honor your loved one is by participating in acts of service or philanthropy in their name. This could involve volunteering for a cause that was important to them, donating to a charity in their honor, or participating in community service projects that reflect their values and passions. By giving back in your loved one's name, you can create a lasting legacy that honors their memory and makes a positive impact on the world.

Additionally, consider incorporating rituals and traditions into your life that help you feel connected to your loved one. This could involve celebrating special occasions or holidays in their honor, observing anniversaries or milestones, or participating in religious or cultural rituals that hold significance for you and your family. By keeping these traditions alive, you can maintain a sense of continuity and connection with your loved one, even as you navigate through your grief.

Finally, remember that there is no right or wrong way to honor your loved one's memory. The most important thing is to find ways to keep their memory alive in your heart and to find comfort and healing in the love and connection you shared. By honoring your loved one in meaningful ways, you can find solace and strength as you navigate the journey of grief.

- The importance of self-care and self-compassion during times of grief

Grief, in its various forms, can drain our emotional, physical, and mental resources. During this challenging time, self-care and self-compassion become essential tools for navigating the pain and fostering healing. Here's why they are so important:

1. Self-Care: Recharging Your Batteries

I. Resilience and Strength: Prioritizing self-care practices like healthy eating, adequate sleep, and regular exercise strengthens your physical and emotional resilience. This allows you to better cope with the demands of grieving and the challenges that may arise.

II. Reduces Stress and Burnout: Grief can be overwhelming, leading to stress and exhaustion. Self-care activities like relaxation techniques, spending time in nature, or engaging in hobbies can help manage stress and prevent burnout.

III. Improved Emotional Well-being: Taking care of yourself doesn't just impact the physical; it also affects your emotional well-being. Engaging in activities you enjoy can boost your mood, offer a sense of accomplishment, and provide a source of joy amidst the pain.

2. Self-Compassion: Recognizing and Embracing Your Needs

I. Validating Your Emotions: Grief is a natural response to loss, and all your emotions, whether sadness, anger, guilt, or fear, are valid. Self-compassion encourages you to acknowledge these emotions without judgment and with understanding.

II. Preventing Self-Criticism: Grief can be isolating and lead to negative self-talk. Self-compassion encourages you to be kind and gentle with yourself during this difficult time. Avoid self-criticism and instead offer yourself the same support and understanding you would extend to a loved one in similar circumstances.

III. Enhances Healing: By practicing self-compassion, you create a space for your emotions to be heard and acknowledged, which can ultimately promote the healing process.

Furthermore, self-care and self-compassion work hand-in-hand during grief. Self-care practices provide the tools to nurture your well-being, while self-compassion creates the space to acknowledge and address your emotional needs with kindness and understanding. By embracing both, you build a foundation for navigating the complexities of grief and fostering healing over time.

It is important to note that, self-care and self-compassion are not selfish acts; they are essential acts of love and respect towards yourself. By prioritizing your well-being and treating yourself with kindness, you empower yourself to navigate the challenging journey of grief and emerge stronger on the other side.

Chapter 3: Transforming Loss to Peace

Transforming loss into peace is a profound journey of healing and growth that involves navigating the complexities of grief with compassion, resilience, and acceptance. It's about finding meaning, connection, and a sense of peace amidst the pain and sorrow of loss.

At its core, transforming loss into peace begins with acknowledging and honoring the depth of your grief. It's about allowing yourself to fully experience the range of emotions that come with loss – from sadness and anger to guilt and confusion – without judgment or suppression. By embracing your grief with openness and vulnerability, you create space for healing and transformation to take place.

Finding meaning in your grief journey is another essential aspect of transforming loss into peace. This involves searching for purpose and understanding in the midst of your pain –

whether it's through reflecting on the lessons learned from your loss, finding ways to honor your loved one's memory, or discovering new sources of strength and resilience within yourself. By finding meaning in your grief, you can begin to see your loss as a catalyst for growth and self-discovery, rather than simply a source of pain and suffering.

Cultivating gratitude is also key to transforming loss into peace. It's about shifting your focus away from what you've lost and towards the blessings that remain – the memories you shared, the love you experienced, and the lessons you learned. By embracing gratitude for the time you had with your loved one and the impact they had on your life, you can find moments of light and joy amidst the darkness of grief.

Practicing forgiveness is another important aspect of transforming loss into peace. This involves releasing any feelings of guilt, anger, or resentment that may be holding you back from finding peace. Whether it's forgiving yourself for things left unsaid or undone, or forgiving others for their perceived shortcomings or mistakes, forgiveness allows you to let go of the past and move forward with compassion and acceptance.

Connecting with others who have experienced similar losses can also be incredibly healing. Sharing your experiences openly and honestly, and receiving support and understanding from those who have walked a similar path, can provide solace and strength during the darkest days of grief. By connecting with others who truly understand your pain, you can find comfort and companionship in shared understanding and empathy.

Another crucial aspect of transforming loss into peace is allowing yourself to engage in rituals and practices that honor the memory of your loved one. These rituals can serve as anchors of remembrance and sources of comfort as you navigate through your grief journey.

Rituals can take many forms, from simple daily practices to more elaborate ceremonies. Lighting a candle in honor of your loved one, visiting their favorite place, or writing letters to them can provide moments of connection and solace. Participating in religious or cultural traditions that hold significance for you and your loved one can also be a meaningful way to honor their memory and find comfort in shared beliefs and practices.

Creating a memorial or tribute in honor of your loved one can also be a powerful way to keep their memory alive. This could involve planting a tree or garden, creating a photo album or scrapbook, or dedicating a special space in your home to display mementos and keepsakes. By creating tangible reminders of your loved one, you can find solace in knowing that their presence continues to be felt and cherished.

Additionally, finding ways to incorporate your loved one's values and passions into your own life can be a meaningful way to honor their memory and find peace in your grief. Whether it's volunteering for a cause they cared about, pursuing a hobby or interest they enjoyed, or carrying on a tradition they started, incorporating their legacy into your life can help you feel connected to them and find purpose in their absence.

Also, engaging in rituals and practices that honor the memory of your loved one allows you to keep their spirit alive in your heart and find comfort in the knowledge that they will always be with you in spirit. By embracing these rituals with love and intention, you can transform your grief into a source of strength and peace that honors the enduring bond you shared with your loved one.

Another aspect to consider in transforming loss into peace is the importance of finding moments of stillness and reflection amidst the chaos of grief. In the midst of overwhelming emotions and upheaval, carving out time for quiet contemplation can provide a much-needed respite and offer clarity and insight.

Taking moments of stillness allows you to pause, breathe, and connect with your inner self. Whether it's through meditation, prayer, or simply sitting in silence, these practices can help you cultivate a sense of peace and inner calm. In these moments, you may find clarity and perspective that can help you navigate the challenges of grief with greater ease and grace.

Moreover, reflection can be a powerful tool for processing your emotions and gaining insight into your grief journey. Journaling, writing letters to your loved one, or engaging in creative expression can provide a space for you to explore your feelings, memories, and experiences in a safe and supportive way. Through reflection, you may uncover hidden strengths, insights, and wisdom that can guide you forward on your path to healing.

Finding moments of stillness and reflection amidst grief is not about avoiding or suppressing your emotions, but rather about creating space to honor and explore them in a gentle and compassionate way. By allowing yourself to be present with your feelings and experiences, you can cultivate a deeper understanding of yourself and your grief, and find peace in the midst of the storm.

Incorporating moments of stillness and reflection into your daily routine can provide a source of comfort and stability as you navigate the ups and downs of grief. Whether it's a few minutes of meditation in the morning, a quiet walk in nature, or an evening ritual of reflection before bed, finding ways to cultivate moments of stillness and reflection can help you find peace and solace amidst the pain of loss.

Finally, embracing self-care and well-being is essential to transforming loss into peace. It's about prioritizing your own physical, emotional, and spiritual needs as you navigate the challenges of grief. Whether it's taking time to rest and recharge, engaging in activities that bring you joy and comfort, or seeking out professional support and guidance, self-care allows you to cultivate a foundation of inner peace and resilience that will carry you through the ups and downs of grief.

- How to transform devastating grief into active and practical love

Transforming devastating grief into active and practical love is a profound process that involves harnessing the intense emotions of loss and redirecting them towards positive actions and meaningful connections. It's about finding purpose and meaning in the midst of pain and using that energy to create a ripple effect of love and compassion in the world.

At its core, this transformation begins with acknowledging and accepting the reality of your grief. It's about allowing yourself to fully experience the depth of your emotions – the sadness, anger, guilt, and despair – without judgment or suppression. By embracing your grief with openness and vulnerability, you create space for healing and growth to occur.

From this place of acceptance, you can begin to channel your grief into positive action. This may involve finding ways to honor the memory of your loved one through acts of service and kindness. Whether it's volunteering for a cause they cared about, participating in charitable events in their honor, or starting a fundraiser or scholarship in their name, these actions allow you to create a lasting legacy that honors their life and values.

In addition to honoring your loved one's memory, transforming grief into love involves practicing compassion towards yourself and others. It's about showing kindness and understanding towards yourself as you navigate the challenges of grief, and extending that same compassion to others who are struggling with their own losses. By reaching out to friends, family members, or support groups who may be in need of support, you create a supportive community of love and understanding that helps ease the pain of grief for everyone involved.

Creating meaningful connections with others who have experienced similar losses is also an important aspect of this transformation. Sharing your journey of grief with others who understand your pain and can offer empathy and support can provide a sense of camaraderie and understanding that helps alleviate feelings of isolation and loneliness. By connecting with others in this way, you can find strength and support in shared experiences of loss, and together, you can navigate the journey of grief with greater resilience and grace.

Engaging in acts of kindness and spreading love and positivity in your daily life is another powerful way to transform grief into love. Whether it's through small gestures of kindness towards strangers, acts of generosity towards friends and family, or volunteering your time and talents to help those in need, these actions allow you to make a positive impact in the world and uplift others during difficult times.

Expressing your love and gratitude towards the people in your life who bring you comfort and support is also essential in this transformation. Taking time to write letters, make phone calls, or simply spend quality time with loved ones, expressing your appreciation for their presence and their kindness, strengthens your connections and brings comfort and solace during difficult times.

Finally, focusing on your own healing and growth is paramount in transforming grief into love. Nurturing your physical, emotional, and spiritual well-being through self-care practices such as meditation, exercise, and creative expression allows you to process your emotions in a healthy and constructive way. Seeking out professional support and guidance if needed, and allowing yourself to grieve in your own way and at your own pace, fosters personal transformation and positive change.

Let me share a story of Sarah , a woman who experienced devastating grief after losing her husband, James, in a tragic accident. Sarah and James had been together for over twenty years, and his sudden death left her feeling lost, shattered, and overwhelmed by the intensity of her emotions.

In the early days of her grief, Sarah found herself consumed by sadness, anger, and despair. She struggled to make sense of her loss and wondered how she would ever find a way forward without James by her side. The pain of her grief was almost unbearable, and she felt as though she would never be able to move past it.

However, as time passed, Sarah began to find moments of solace and comfort in unexpected places. She discovered that by honoring James's memory and channeling her grief into positive actions, she could transform her pain into a powerful force for love and compassion in the world.

Sarah started by volunteering at a local charity that James had been passionate about. She dedicated her time and energy to helping others in need, knowing that this was a cause that would have mattered deeply to him. Through her acts of service, Sarah found a sense of purpose and meaning that helped ease the pain of her grief and bring a sense of fulfillment to her life.

In addition to her volunteer work, Sarah also reached out to others who were struggling with their own losses. She joined a support group for widows and widowers and found comfort in sharing her experiences with others who understood her pain. By offering empathy and understanding to those who were going through similar struggles, Sarah found strength and solace in the connections she formed with others.

Sarah also made a conscious effort to practice self-care and self-compassion as she navigated the challenges of grief. She allowed herself to grieve in her own way and at her own pace, without judgment or self-criticism. She prioritized her physical, emotional, and spiritual well-being, engaging in activities that brought her comfort and solace, such as meditation, yoga, and spending time in nature.

As time went on, Sarah's grief began to transform into something more powerful and life-affirming. Instead of being consumed by her pain, she found herself filled with a deep sense of love and gratitude for the time she had shared with James and the memories they had created together. She realized that by embracing her grief with compassion and acceptance, she could honor James's memory and carry his legacy forward in a meaningful way.

Just like i have been saying earlier, Sarah's journey shows the transformative power of love and compassion in the face of devastating grief. When Sarah lost her husband, James, in a tragic accident, she was plunged into a world of pain and sorrow. The intensity of her grief was overwhelming, and she struggled to imagine a future without James by her side.

However, as Sarah navigated through her grief, she discovered that love could be a guiding light in even the darkest of times. Instead of allowing herself to be consumed by her pain, Sarah made a conscious decision to honor James's memory by channeling her grief into positive actions and meaningful connections.

Through volunteering at a local charity and reaching out to others who were struggling with their own losses, Sarah found purpose and meaning in her grief. She realized that by extending kindness and compassion to others, she could create a ripple effect of love and healing in the world.

At the same time, Sarah prioritized self-care and self-compassion, recognizing the importance of nurturing her own well-being as she navigated through her grief. By allowing herself to grieve in her own way and at her own pace, she created space for healing and growth to occur.

As time went on, Sarah's grief transformed from a source of pain into a powerful force for love and compassion. Instead of being defined by her loss, she found herself filled with gratitude for the time she had shared with James and the love they had shared. Through her acts of kindness and her commitment to honoring James's memory, Sarah discovered that love had the power to transcend even the deepest of sorrows.

In the end, Sarah's journey serves as a reminder that love is the greatest gift we can give, even in the face of loss and adversity. By embracing her grief with compassion and acceptance, Sarah was able to transform her pain into a legacy of love that continues to inspire and uplift others long after James's passing.

- Finding peace and acceptance in the face of loss

Finding peace and acceptance in the face of loss is a deeply personal and transformative journey that involves navigating the complexities of grief with grace and resilience. It's about coming to terms with the reality of our loss, embracing our emotions with compassion and understanding, and finding a sense of peace amidst the pain and sorrow.

Finding peace and acceptance also involves letting go of expectations and timelines for the grieving process. There is no right or wrong way to grieve, and there is no set timeline for how long it should take. Each person's journey of grief is unique, and it's important to allow ourselves the time and space we need to heal in our own way and at our own pace.

Another important aspect of finding peace and acceptance in the face of loss is the practice of forgiveness – both towards ourselves and others. Forgiveness is a powerful tool for releasing the emotional burdens that can weigh us down during the grieving process.

Forgiving ourselves involves letting go of any guilt or self-blame we may be carrying related to our loved one's death or our actions leading up to it. It's about recognizing that we are only human and that we did the best we could with the knowledge and resources we had at the time. By offering ourselves forgiveness, we can free ourselves from the cycle of self-judgment and find a sense of peace and acceptance within.

Similarly, forgiving others who may have played a role in our loved one's death or who may have hurt us in some way during our grief journey can also be incredibly healing. It's not about condoning or excusing their actions, but rather about releasing the anger, resentment, and bitterness that may be holding us back from finding peace and acceptance. By choosing to forgive others, we open ourselves up to greater compassion, understanding, and connection with ourselves and with those around us.

In addition to forgiveness, another crucial aspect of finding peace and acceptance in the face of loss is the cultivation of resilience. Resilience is the ability to bounce back from adversity, to adapt to change, and to grow stronger in the face of challenges. While grief can feel overwhelming and debilitating, developing resilience can help us navigate through the pain and find a sense of peace and acceptance on the other side.

One way to cultivate resilience is by fostering a sense of hope and optimism, even in the midst of our darkest moments. This involves believing in our ability to overcome adversity, to find meaning in our experiences, and to create a fulfilling life in spite of our loss. By cultivating a positive outlook and focusing on the possibilities for growth and transformation, we can build resilience and find a sense of peace and acceptance in the face of loss.

Another important aspect of resilience is building a strong support network of friends, family, and community members who can offer understanding, empathy, and encouragement during times of grief. By surrounding ourselves with people who care about us and who are willing to support us through our pain, we can find strength and solace in our connections with others.

Additionally, another significant aspect of finding peace and acceptance in the face of loss is the practice of mindfulness and presence. Mindfulness involves bringing our full attention to the present moment with an attitude of openness, curiosity, and non-judgment. In the midst of grief, our minds may be consumed by thoughts of the past – replaying memories of our loved one or dwelling on regrets and what-ifs –

or by worries about the future – fearing a life without them or dreading more loss.

However, by cultivating mindfulness, we can learn to anchor ourselves in the present moment, finding solace and acceptance in what is here and now. This allows us to observe our thoughts and emotions with compassion, without getting swept away by them. It helps us to acknowledge the reality of our loss without being overwhelmed by it, and to find moments of peace and acceptance amidst the storm of grief.

Practicing mindfulness can take many forms, from meditation and deep breathing exercises to mindful movement practices like yoga or tai chi. It can also be as simple as taking a few moments each day to pause, breathe, and notice the sensations of our breath, the sights and sounds around us, and the feelings in our body and heart. By bringing our attention back to the present moment, we can find refuge from the pain of the past and the uncertainty of the future, and discover a sense of peace and acceptance that transcends our grief.

Moreover, mindfulness can also help us cultivate gratitude and appreciation for the blessings that remain in our lives, even in the midst of loss. By focusing on what we are grateful for – whether it's the love and support of friends and family, the beauty of nature, or the simple joys of everyday life – we can shift our perspective from one of loss and scarcity to one of abundance and gratitude. This doesn't diminish the pain of our grief, but it can help us find moments of peace and acceptance amidst the pain, and remind us that there is still goodness and beauty to be found in the world.

- Honoring your loved one's memory through love and compassion

Honoring your loved one's memory through love and compassion is a deeply meaningful way to keep their spirit alive and create a lasting legacy of their presence in your life. It involves actively incorporating their values, teachings, and the love you shared into your daily actions and interactions with others.

One way to honor your loved one's memory is by embodying the qualities they exemplified in their life, such as kindness, generosity, and empathy. By striving to emulate these traits in your own interactions with others, you not only honor their memory but also carry forward their legacy of love and compassion.

Additionally, another meaningful way to honor your loved one's memory through love and compassion is by creating a legacy project or initiative in their honor. This could involve starting a foundation, scholarship, or charitable fund in their name, dedicated to causes or organizations that were important to them or that align with their values and passions.

By establishing a legacy project, you create a lasting tribute to your loved one's life and legacy, while also making a positive impact in the world. Whether it's supporting education, healthcare, environmental conservation, or other causes close to their heart, a legacy project allows you to honor their memory in a tangible and meaningful way.

Moreover, involving others in the legacy project – whether it's friends, family members, or members of the community – can help amplify its impact and create a sense of shared purpose and connection. By rallying support and participation from others who knew and loved your loved one, you can create a legacy that extends far beyond your own circle of influence and leaves a lasting impact on the world.

In addition to creating a legacy project, you can also honor your loved one's memory by continuing their passions and interests in your own life. Whether it's pursuing hobbies or activities they enjoyed, carrying on traditions they started, or advocating for causes they were passionate about, finding ways to incorporate their legacy into your own life allows you to keep their spirit alive and create a sense of continuity and connection with them.

Furthermore, sharing stories and memories of your loved one with others can help keep their memory alive and create connections with those who knew and loved them. Whether it's through writing letters, creating scrapbooks or photo albums, or simply reminiscing with friends and family, sharing memories of your loved one allows you to celebrate their life and the impact they had on those around them.

Another meaningful way to honor your loved one's memory through love and compassion is by creating a space or memorial dedicated to them. This could be a physical space, such as a garden, bench, or plaque, or a virtual space, such as a website or online memorial page.

Creating a physical or virtual memorial provides a tangible way to honor your loved one's memory and create a space for reflection and remembrance. It allows you and others who knew and loved them to come together to share stories, memories, and tributes, keeping their spirit alive in a meaningful and lasting way.

A physical memorial, such as a garden or bench in a favorite spot, provides a peaceful and serene space for quiet reflection and remembrance. It can serve as a place of solace and comfort for you and others who visit, allowing you to feel close to your loved one and find moments of peace and connection.

A virtual memorial, on the other hand, offers a digital space for sharing memories, photos, and messages of love and support. It provides a platform for friends and family members from near and far to come together to celebrate your loved one's life and legacy, regardless of physical distance.

Whether physical or virtual, creating a space or memorial dedicated to your loved one allows you to honor their memory in a meaningful and personal way. It provides a place for healing, reflection, and connection, and serves as a lasting tribute to the impact they had on your life and the lives of others.

Chapter 4: Moving Through Grief

Moving through grief is a deeply personal and transformative journey that involves navigating through the pain, confusion, and emotions that accompany loss. While grief is a natural response to loss, it can also feel overwhelming and confusing, leaving us feeling lost and unsure of how to move forward.

One of the first steps in moving through grief is acknowledging and accepting the reality of our loss. This involves allowing ourselves to fully experience the emotions that come with grief – whether it's sadness, anger, guilt, or confusion – without judgment or suppression. By acknowledging our grief and allowing ourselves to feel it, we create space for healing and growth to occur.

As we navigate through grief, it's important to be gentle and compassionate with ourselves. This means giving ourselves permission to grieve in our own way and at our own pace, without comparing ourselves to others or feeling pressured to "get over" our loss. Grief is a journey, not a destination, and it's okay to take as much time as we need to heal.

Finding support from others can also be incredibly helpful in moving through grief. Whether it's friends, family members, support groups, or mental health professionals, having a supportive network of people who understand and empathize with our pain can provide comfort and solace during difficult times. Talking about our feelings, sharing memories of our loved one, and seeking professional help when needed can all help us navigate through grief with greater ease and resilience.

Another important aspect of moving through grief is finding healthy ways to express and process our emotions. Grief can bring up a wide range of feelings, from sadness and anger to guilt and regret, and it's important to find outlets for these emotions in order to release them in a healthy way.

One way to express and process our emotions is through creative outlets such as writing, art, music, or poetry. These mediums provide a safe and cathartic way to explore our feelings and experiences, allowing us to express ourselves in ways that words alone may not be able to capture. Whether it's journaling about our memories and emotions, creating art that reflects our innermost thoughts and feelings, or writing songs or poems as a form of self-expression, creative outlets can provide a powerful means of processing grief and finding healing and solace in the process.

In addition to creative outlets, physical activity can also be an effective way to release pent-up emotions and tension associated with grief. Whether it's going for a walk or run, practicing yoga or tai chi, or engaging in sports or other forms of exercise, physical activity can help us release stress and tension, boost our mood, and promote a sense of well-being and inner peace. Movement can also be a way of connecting with our bodies and accessing emotions that may be difficult to express verbally, allowing us to process our grief on a deeper level.

Furthermore, finding ways to connect with our spirituality or faith can provide comfort and solace as we navigate through grief. Whether it's through prayer, meditation, attending religious or spiritual services, or seeking guidance from spiritual leaders or mentors, connecting with our spiritual beliefs and practices can offer a sense of hope, meaning, and support during difficult times. Spiritual practices can provide a framework for understanding and making sense of our loss, and can offer a sense of connection to something greater than ourselves, helping us find peace and acceptance in the midst of grief.

Alright, let's dissect everything using a session I had with one of my clients, discussing how she has been coping with grief.

Therapist: Hello, Sarah. It's good to see you again. How have you been since our last session?

Client (Sarah): Hi, I've been managing. Some days are better than others, you know?

Therapist: Absolutely, grief has its ups and downs. How have you been coping with everything?

Sarah: Well, I've been trying to stay busy and keep my mind occupied. I've been spending more time with friends and family, which helps distract me from the pain sometimes.

Therapist: That sounds like a good way to stay connected and supported. Have you noticed any changes in how you're feeling since we last spoke?

Sarah: Yeah, I think I've been feeling a little more accepting of everything. I still miss him terribly, but I'm starting to come to terms with the fact that he's gone.

Therapist: It's a big step to accept the reality of loss. How have you been able to work through your grief?

Sarah: Well, I've been trying to allow myself to feel whatever comes up, without judging it or pushing it away. I've also been doing some journaling and creative writing, which seems to help me process my emotions.

Therapist: Journaling can be a powerful tool for processing grief. Is there anything else you've found helpful in moving through your grief?

Sarah: I've been trying to focus on self-care and self-compassion. I've been making more time for things that nourish me, like going for walks in nature and practicing mindfulness meditation.

Therapist: That's wonderful to hear. Taking care of yourself is so important, especially during times of grief. Have you noticed any shifts in your perspective or outlook on life as you've moved through your grief journey?

Sarah: Definitely. I think I've become more grateful for the time I had with him and the memories we shared. And I've started to see that even though he's gone, his love and his presence still live on in me and in the world around me.

Therapist: That's a beautiful insight, Sarah. It sounds like you're making progress in finding peace and acceptance amidst your grief.

Sarah: Thank you. It's still a work in progress, but I'm taking it one day at a time.I've also been exploring new ways to honor my husband's memory. I've started volunteering at a local animal shelter because he was passionate about animal welfare. It feels good to give back in a way that's meaningful to him.

Therapist: That's a beautiful way to honor his memory and keep his spirit alive. How does it feel to engage in activities that connect you to him in that way?

Sarah: It's bittersweet, to be honest. There's a sense of joy and fulfillment in doing something that he would have loved, but there's also a pang of sadness that he's not here to share it with me.

But overall, it's been a positive experience that's helped me feel closer to him in some ways.

Therapist: It's understandable to feel a mix of emotions when engaging in activities that remind you of your husband. It sounds like you're finding a balance between honoring his memory and allowing yourself to feel your emotions fully.

Sarah: Yeah, I think that's been key for me – allowing myself to feel the full spectrum of emotions without trying to suppress or ignore them. It's not always easy, but I think it's important for my healing process.

Therapist: Absolutely. Acknowledging and processing your emotions is an important part of moving through grief. Is there anything else you've been doing to cope with your loss?

Sarah: Well, I've also been seeking out opportunities for growth and self-discovery. I've been taking classes and workshops that I've always been interested in but never had the courage to pursue before. It's been empowering to step out of my comfort zone and explore new facets of myself.

Therapist: That's fantastic, Sarah. It sounds like you're finding ways to channel your grief into personal growth and transformation. How has this journey of self-discovery been for you?

Sarah: It's been eye-opening, to say the least. I think losing my husband has made me realize the importance of living life to the fullest and not taking anything for granted. It's pushed me to step outside of my comfort zone and embrace new experiences, even if they're scary at first.

Therapist: It's inspiring to hear how you're finding meaning and purpose in the midst of your grief. Remember, I'm here to support you as you continue on this journey of healing and self-discovery.

Sarah: Thank you, I appreciate that. It's comforting to know that I have someone to talk to who understands what I'm going through.

Therapist: Of course, Sarah. You're not alone in this journey. We'll get through it together.

This interaction captures the complexity of Sarah's grief journey – the moments of joy and connection, the challenges of facing her emotions, and the courage and resilience she displays as she embarks on a journey of healing and self-discovery.

- The importance of allowing yourself to grieve fully and authentically

The importance of allowing yourself to grieve fully and authentically cannot be overstated. Grief is a natural response to loss, whether it's the death of a loved one, the end of a relationship, or any other significant change or transition in life. Suppressing or denying our grief only prolongs the healing process and can lead to further emotional distress in the long run.

When we allow ourselves to grieve fully and authentically, we give ourselves permission to experience the wide range of emotions that accompany loss – sadness, anger, guilt, confusion, and more. These emotions are all valid and important parts of the grieving process, and denying them only serves to bottle up our feelings, which can eventually manifest in physical or mental health issues.

By allowing ourselves to grieve fully, we create space for healing and transformation to occur. Grief is a journey, not a destination, and it takes time to navigate through the pain and come to terms with our loss. By honoring our emotions and allowing ourselves to feel them fully, we give ourselves the opportunity to process our feelings, gain insight and understanding, and ultimately find a sense of peace and acceptance.

Moreover, allowing ourselves to grieve fully and authentically also opens the door to connection and support from others. When we're honest and vulnerable about our grief, we invite others to share in our journey and offer their empathy, understanding, and support. This sense of connection can be incredibly comforting and validating, and it reminds us that we're not alone in our pain.

Allowing yourself to grieve fully and authentically also honors the significance of the loss in your life. Whether it's the loss of a loved one, a job, a dream, or an aspect of your identity, acknowledging the impact of the loss is a crucial step in the healing process. By allowing yourself to fully experience your grief, you validate the significance of what has been lost and give yourself permission to mourn its absence.

Furthermore, allowing yourself to grieve fully and authentically fosters resilience and emotional growth. Grief has the potential to teach us valuable lessons about life, love, and the human experience. By embracing our grief and allowing ourselves to learn from it, we can emerge from the experience with a deeper sense of compassion, empathy, and wisdom.

In addition, allowing yourself to grieve fully and authentically sets an important example for others. By openly acknowledging and expressing your grief, you give permission for those around you to do the same. This creates a culture of openness and support, where individuals feel safe to share their emotions and seek help when needed.

Additionally, allowing yourself to grieve fully and authentically can lead to a deeper understanding of yourself and your own inner resilience. Through the process of grieving, you may uncover hidden strengths, resources, and coping mechanisms that you didn't know you possessed. As you navigate through the pain and turmoil of grief, you may discover new facets of your identity and experience personal growth and transformation.

Moreover, allowing yourself to grieve fully and authentically can pave the way for meaningful connections with others who have experienced similar losses. Sharing your grief openly and honestly can create bonds of empathy and understanding with others, fostering a sense of community and support that is invaluable during difficult times. By allowing yourself to be vulnerable and authentic in your grief, you create opportunities for deep and meaningful connections with others who can offer comfort, companionship, and solidarity along the journey.

Ultimately, allowing yourself to grieve fully and authentically is an act of courage and self-compassion that honors the depth of your emotions and experiences. It is a vital step in the healing process that can lead to profound personal growth, deeper connections with others, and a renewed sense of purpose and meaning in life.

- Cherishing the memories of your loved one while still moving forward in life

Cherishing the memories of your loved one while still moving forward in life is a delicate balancing act that requires honoring the past while embracing the future. It's about finding a way to hold onto the love, laughter, and special moments shared with your loved one, while also allowing yourself to open up to new experiences and opportunities for growth.

One way to cherish the memories of your loved one is by finding ways to incorporate their presence into special occasions and milestones. This could include setting a place for them at the dinner table during holidays, lighting a candle in their honor on significant anniversaries, or finding symbolic ways to include them in important life events, such as weddings, graduations, or the birth of a child. By finding meaningful ways to include your loved one in these moments, you ensure that their memory continues to be a cherished part of your life and the lives of those around you.

At the same time, it's important to allow yourself to move forward and embrace the future with hope and optimism. This doesn't mean forgetting about your loved one or replacing them in your heart, but rather recognizing that life goes on and that it's okay to find joy and fulfillment in new experiences and relationships.

Finding a balance between cherishing the memories of your loved one and moving forward in life may involve navigating feelings of guilt or sadness. It's natural to feel conflicted about experiencing happiness or moving on without your loved one by your side. However, honoring their memory doesn't mean being stuck in the past or holding onto grief indefinitely. It means finding a way to integrate their presence into your life in a way that allows you to live fully and authentically.

Let me tell you a story to illustrate the concept of cherishing memories while moving forward in life:

Emily lost her husband, David, unexpectedly to a sudden illness. They had been married for 25 years and shared a deep bond built on love, laughter, and mutual respect. David was an avid gardener and spent countless hours cultivating their backyard garden, which had become a sanctuary for both of them.

After David's passing, Emily found solace in spending time in the garden, surrounded by the plants and flowers he had nurtured with such care. It became a sacred space where she could feel close to him and remember the happy moments they had shared together.

As Emily navigated her grief journey, she decided to create a dedicated memorial in the garden to honor David's memory. She set up a bench under the shade of their favorite tree and adorned it with a plaque inscribed with his name and a quote that captured his essence. Surrounding the bench, Emily planted flowers and shrubs that David had loved, creating a vibrant and colorful tribute to his life.

The garden memorial became a cherished space for Emily and her family to come together and remember David. They would gather there on special occasions and anniversaries to share stories, shed tears, and find comfort in each other's presence. Emily also established a tradition of lighting a candle at the memorial on David's birthday, a simple yet meaningful ritual that allowed her to feel close to him and honor his memory.

In addition to the physical memorial, Emily found other ways to cherish David's memory while moving forward in life. She started a community garden project in his honor, where volunteers would come together to tend to the garden and donate the produce to local food banks. Through this project, Emily not only honored David's passion for gardening but also made a positive impact in their community, spreading joy and nourishment in his name.

By creating a dedicated memorial and engaging in meaningful activities to honor David's memory, Emily found a way to cherish his presence while still moving forward in life. The garden became a symbol of love, resilience, and healing, a tangible reminder of the enduring bond they shared and the beauty that David brought into her life. And through her actions and endeavors, Emily ensured that David's legacy continued to shine brightly, touching the lives of others in meaningful and lasting ways.

Let's also consider the story of Sarah, a mother who tragically lost her teenage son, Alex, in a car accident. Alex was Sarah's only child, and their bond was incredibly strong. They shared a love for hiking and exploring the outdoors together, and some of their fondest memories were made on hiking trails and camping trips.

After Alex's passing, Sarah was overwhelmed with grief. She struggled to come to terms with the sudden and senseless loss of her beloved son. Every corner of their home seemed to hold memories of him, from the photos on the walls to the hiking gear in the garage.

As Sarah navigated her grief journey, she found solace in revisiting the places they had loved to explore together. She would often hike the same trails they had once traversed hand in hand, taking comfort in the familiar sights and sounds of nature that reminded her of Alex's presence.

One day, while hiking along their favorite trail, Sarah stumbled upon a secluded clearing with a breathtaking view of the mountains. Inspired by the serenity and beauty of the spot, she decided to create a memorial in honor of Alex. She cleared away the brush and debris, creating a small space where she could sit and reflect on her son's life and the memories they had shared.

Sarah adorned the memorial with a plaque inscribed with Alex's name and a quote that captured his adventurous spirit. She also planted wildflowers around the clearing, choosing species that bloomed in vibrant colors throughout the year. As the seasons changed, the memorial became a kaleidoscope of color, a living tribute to Alex's vibrant personality and zest for life.

The memorial clearing became a sacred space for Sarah to connect with her son's spirit and cherish his memory. She would visit the spot regularly, sometimes alone and sometimes with friends and family who wanted to pay their respects. Together, they would share stories and memories of Alex, finding comfort and healing in each other's presence.

In addition to the physical memorial, Sarah found other ways to honor Alex's memory while moving forward in life. She started a scholarship fund in his name, providing financial assistance to students who shared his passion for outdoor adventure and exploration. She also became an advocate for road safety, sharing Alex's story to raise awareness about the dangers of distracted driving and promote safer driving practices in her community.

By creating a dedicated memorial and engaging in meaningful activities to honor Alex's memory, Sarah found a way to cherish his presence while still moving forward in life. The memorial clearing became a symbol of love, resilience, and healing, a tangible reminder of the enduring bond they shared and the beauty that Alex brought into her life. And through her actions and endeavors, Sarah ensured that Alex's legacy continued to shine brightly, touching the lives of others in meaningful and lasting ways.

- Understanding that grief is a lifelong journey, but one that can be filled with love and beauty

Understanding that grief is a lifelong journey, but one that can be filled with love and beauty, is a perspective that acknowledges the complexity of the grieving process while embracing the potential for healing and growth.

Grief is not something that can be neatly packaged and put away; rather, it is a journey that unfolds over time, with its own ebbs and flows, twists and turns. It's a journey that can be marked by moments of profound sadness and longing, as well as moments of unexpected beauty and joy.

While the pain of loss may never fully disappear, over time, it can become integrated into our lives in a way that allows us to find meaning, purpose, and even beauty in our experiences of grief. We may discover new depths of compassion and empathy within ourselves as we navigate the complexities of loss. We may find solace and comfort in the memories of our loved ones, cherishing the moments we shared and the impact they had on our lives.

Moreover, grief has the potential to deepen our connections with others and enrich our relationships. Through our shared experiences of loss, we may find a sense of solidarity and understanding with others who have walked a similar path. We may find strength and support in our connections with friends, family, and community members who stand by us in our moments of sorrow and celebration.

In addition, grief can inspire us to live more fully and authentically, cherishing each moment and embracing the beauty and wonder of life. We may find ourselves drawn to activities and experiences that bring us joy and fulfillment, whether it's spending time in nature, pursuing creative passions, or nurturing meaningful relationships. We may find a renewed sense of purpose and gratitude as we navigate the complexities of loss and love.

Furthermore, understanding that grief is a lifelong journey filled with love and beauty involves embracing the idea that our loved ones continue to live on through us and the legacies they leave behind. While they may no longer be physically present, their presence remains alive in our hearts, memories, and the ways in which they have touched our lives.

Moreover, understanding that grief is a lifelong journey invites us to cultivate a sense of mindfulness and presence in our lives. It encourages us to be fully present in each moment, savoring the beauty and joy that surrounds us, even in the midst of sorrow. By embracing life with open hearts and minds, we can find moments of peace, connection, and gratitude that sustain us on our journey of grief and remembrance.

Additionally, understanding that grief is a lifelong journey, but one that can be filled with love and beauty, invites us to embrace the concept of continuing bonds with our loved ones who have passed away. Rather than viewing death as an ending, we can choose to see it as a transformation of the relationship, where our connection with our loved ones evolves rather than ceases.

Continuing bonds acknowledge that even though our loved ones may no longer be physically present, they remain a significant part of our lives. We may continue to feel their presence, hear their voice, or sense their guidance in our daily lives. This can manifest in various ways, such as through dreams, signs or symbols, or a sense of intuition or inner knowing.

By embracing the idea of continuing bonds, we open ourselves up to the possibility of maintaining an ongoing relationship with our loved ones, even after they have passed away. This can provide comfort, reassurance, and a sense of connection as we navigate the ups and downs of life.

Furthermore, understanding that grief is a lifelong journey filled with love and beauty encourages us to cultivate self-compassion and self-care along the way. It's important to recognize that grief can be physically, emotionally, and mentally exhausting, and that it's okay to prioritize our own well-being as we navigate the grieving process.

Ultimately, understanding that grief is a lifelong journey filled with love and beauty is about finding meaning and purpose in our experiences of loss. It's about embracing the full spectrum of human emotion, from the depths of sorrow to the heights of joy, and recognizing that each moment is an opportunity for growth, healing, and connection. By embracing this perspective, we can find comfort and solace in the midst of grief, and cultivate a sense of resilience, hope, and love that sustains us on our journey through life.

Chapter 5: Supporting Others Through Grief

Supporting others through grief is a delicate and different process that involves providing comfort, empathy, and practical assistance to those who are mourning the loss of a loved one. It requires a deep understanding of the individual's unique experiences, emotions, and needs, as well as a willingness to offer unconditional support and companionship during a time of profound sadness and vulnerability.

One of the most important aspects of supporting others through grief is listening with empathy. This means being fully present and attentive to the grieving individual's words, feelings, and emotions without judgment or interruption. It involves creating a safe and non-judgmental space where they can freely express their thoughts and emotions without fear of being dismissed or invalidated. By actively listening to their stories, memories, and feelings, you validate their experiences and provide a sense of comfort and validation during a challenging time.

In addition to listening, offering practical support can be immensely helpful for someone who is grieving. This may involve helping with daily tasks and responsibilities, such as running errands, preparing meals, or taking care of household chores. By offering tangible assistance, you alleviate some of the burdens that the grieving individual may be facing, allowing them to focus on their emotional healing and well-being.

Furthermore, acknowledging the significance of the loss and validating the grieving individual's emotions is crucial for providing meaningful support. This involves using empathetic and compassionate language to express your condolences and support, such as "I'm here for you," "I'm so sorry for your loss," or "I can't imagine what you're going through." By acknowledging their pain and expressing your support, you create a sense of connection and understanding that can provide immense comfort during a time of profound sadness and loss.

Respecting the grieving individual's process and timeline is also essential for providing effective support. Grief is a highly individual and personal experience, and everyone processes it differently. It's important to avoid imposing your own expectations or judgments onto the grieving individual and instead, allow them to grieve in their own way and at their own pace. This may involve being patient and understanding, even if their grief manifests in ways that may seem unfamiliar or uncomfortable to you.

Offering resources and follow-up support can also be valuable for someone who is grieving. Providing information about support groups, counseling services, or other resources can empower them to seek the help they need to navigate their grief journey. Additionally, following up with the grieving individual in the days, weeks, and months following their loss shows that you care and that you are there to offer support and companionship for the long haul.

In addition to the aforementioned aspects, validating the grieving individual's emotions and experiences is paramount in providing meaningful support through grief. This entails acknowledging the complexity of their feelings, which may include a range of emotions such as sadness, anger, guilt, and even relief. By validating their emotions and experiences, you convey acceptance and understanding, reassuring them that their feelings are normal and valid given the circumstances.

Moreover, offering reassurance and encouragement can be instrumental in supporting someone through grief. Remind them that it's okay to feel whatever emotions they are experiencing and that there is no "right" or "wrong" way to grieve. Encourage them to be gentle with themselves and to prioritize self-care as they navigate their grief journey. Offer words of encouragement and support, reminding them that they are not alone and that you are there to support them every step of the way.

Additionally, practicing patience and flexibility is essential when supporting someone through grief. Grieving is a nonlinear process, and individuals may experience fluctuations in their emotions and needs over time. Be patient and understanding as they navigate the ups and downs of grief, and be flexible in your approach to providing support. Recognize that their needs may change over time, and be willing to adapt your support accordingly to meet them where they are in their grief journey.

Furthermore, maintaining open and honest communication is key to fostering a supportive relationship with someone who is grieving. Encourage them to express their thoughts, feelings, and needs openly and honestly, and be receptive to their communication. Create a safe and non-judgmental space where they feel comfortable sharing their vulnerabilities and concerns, and be willing to listen with an open heart and mind.

Another important aspect of supporting others through grief is respecting their boundaries and autonomy. While it's crucial to offer support and companionship, it's equally important to recognize that each individual may have different needs and preferences when it comes to receiving support.

Respecting boundaries means allowing the grieving individual to set the pace and boundaries for their own healing process. This may involve respecting their need for space and solitude at times, as well as honoring their decisions about when and how they want to talk about their grief. Avoid pressuring them to share more than they are comfortable with or to engage in activities that may feel overwhelming or triggering for them.

Additionally, respecting autonomy means empowering the grieving individual to make their own choices about how they want to navigate their grief journey. Offer support and guidance, but ultimately, allow them to take the lead in deciding what feels right for them. This may involve respecting their decisions about seeking professional help, participating in support groups, or engaging in self-care activities that support their healing process.

By respecting boundaries and autonomy, you demonstrate trust and respect for the grieving individual's ability to navigate their own grief journey in a way that feels authentic and empowering for them. This fosters a sense of agency and self-efficacy, which can be incredibly empowering for someone who is grieving and seeking to find their own path to healing and growth.

Lastly, offering ongoing support and companionship is vital for someone who is grieving. Grief is a lifelong journey, and the grieving individual may continue to need support and companionship long after the initial loss. Check in with them regularly, offer to spend time together, and continue to provide reassurance, encouragement, and validation as they navigate their grief journey. By being a consistent and supportive presence in their life, you can help them feel loved, supported, and understood as they heal and grow through grief.

- How to comfort and support a loved one who is grieving

Comforting and supporting a loved one who is grieving is a deeply empathetic and human process that involves validating their experiences and emotions. This means acknowledging the depth and complexity of their grief and affirming the significance of their loss. It involves using empathetic and validating language to express your understanding and support, such as "I can't imagine what you're going through, but I'm here for you," or "Your feelings are completely valid, and I'm here to support you in any way I can."

In addition to validating their emotions, it's important to offer them opportunities for reminiscence and honoring the memory of their lost loved one. Encouraging them to share stories, memories, and anecdotes about the person they've lost can provide comfort and validation of their relationship. By actively listening to their reminiscences and engaging with their memories, you demonstrate that their loved one's life and legacy continue to hold significance and are worthy of celebration.

Let's consider this conversation between a therapist and a grieving relative ,and also see how they reach out to support their loved ones during their time of grief and the impact ;

Therapist: Hello, thank you for joining me today. How have you been holding up since our last session?

Grieving Relative: Thank you, I've been doing okay. It's been tough, but I'm trying to take things one day at a time.

Therapist: I'm glad to hear that. I know you've been dealing with a lot lately, especially with supporting your niece through her grief. How has that been going?

Grieving Relative: It's been a rollercoaster, to be honest. She's been struggling a lot since losing her mom, my sister. It's been hard to see her in so much pain.

Therapist: It's understandable that it's been difficult for both of you. Can you tell me more about how you've been supporting her through her grief process?

Grieving Relative: Well, I've been trying to be there for her as much as I can. I listen to her when she wants to talk, and I try to validate her feelings and emotions. I've also been helping out with practical things, like running errands and taking care of things around the house so she can have some space to grieve.

Therapist: It sounds like you've been providing her with a lot of emotional and practical support, which is incredibly important during this time. How has she been responding to your support?

Grieving Relative: She seems to appreciate it, but I can tell that she's still struggling. Some days are better than others, but overall, it's been really hard for her to cope with the loss.

Therapist: It's normal for the grieving process to have its ups and downs, and it's important to remember that healing takes time. Have you noticed any specific ways in which your support has been helpful for her?

Grieving Relative: Well, I think just knowing that she's not alone in her grief has been comforting for her. She's told me that she appreciates having someone to talk to who understands what she's going through. And I've noticed that she seems to be opening up more and expressing her feelings, which I think is a positive sign.

Therapist: That's great to hear. It sounds like your presence and support have been incredibly meaningful for her during this challenging time. Just remember to continue to be patient and understanding, and to take care of yourself as well as you support her through her grief journey.

Grieving Relative: Thank you, I'll keep that in mind. It's definitely been a learning process for both of us, but I'm committed to being there for her every step of the way.

Therapist: I have no doubt that your continued support and compassion will make a significant difference in her healing process. If you ever need additional support or guidance, please don't hesitate to reach out. You're doing a wonderful job supporting your niece through her grief, and I'm here to help in any way I can.

The conversation above offers comfort and support to the grieving relative by providing validation, empathy, guidance, and encouragement. Through their words and actions, the therapist helps the relative feel supported and empowered in their role as a caregiver, which can ultimately strengthen their ability to support their loved one through grief.

- The importance of being present and listening without judgment

The importance of being present and listening without judgment cannot be overstated, especially when supporting someone who is grieving. When we are truly present with someone, it means that we are fully engaged and attentive to their needs, emotions, and experiences in that moment. This level of presence communicates to the grieving individual that they are valued, heard, and supported, which can be incredibly comforting during a time of profound sadness and vulnerability.

Listening without judgment is equally essential in providing support through grief. Grieving individuals may experience a wide range of emotions, thoughts, and reactions, some of which may be difficult or uncomfortable to hear. When we listen without judgment, we create a safe and non-judgmental space for them to express themselves openly and honestly, without fear of criticism or condemnation.

By listening without judgment, we validate the grieving individual's experiences and emotions, affirming that their feelings are normal and valid given the circumstances. This validation helps them feel understood and accepted, which can provide immense comfort and reassurance during a time of grief.

Moreover, listening without judgment allows us to truly empathize with the grieving individual, experiencing their pain and sorrow alongside them. This empathetic connection fosters a sense of solidarity and companionship, helping the grieving individual feel less alone in their grief.

In addition to providing comfort and validation, being present and listening without judgment allows for deeper understanding and connection between the supporter and the grieving individual. When we approach the grieving process with an open heart and mind, we create an environment where the person experiencing grief feels safe to explore their emotions, thoughts, and memories without fear of being misunderstood or criticized.

Furthermore, being present and listening without judgment fosters trust and strengthens the bond between the supporter and the grieving individual. When someone feels truly heard and understood, they are more likely to lean on that person for support and confide in them during times of need. This trust and bond are essential for building a supportive relationship that can withstand the challenges of grief.

Moreover, being present and listening without judgment allows the supporter to gain insight into the grieving individual's unique needs, preferences, and coping mechanisms. By understanding the individual's experiences and perspective, the supporter can tailor their support to better meet their needs and provide more effective assistance throughout the grieving process.

Ultimately, being present and listening without judgment are not only acts of compassion and empathy, but they also lay the foundation for a supportive and meaningful relationship between the supporter and the grieving individual. Through these simple yet powerful acts, we can offer comfort, validation, understanding, and support to those who are navigating the difficult journey of grief.

- The power of empathy and understanding in helping others navigate their grief

The power of empathy and understanding in helping others navigate their grief cannot be overstated. When we approach someone who is grieving with genuine empathy and understanding, we create a safe and supportive space for them to express their emotions, thoughts, and experiences without fear of judgment or rejection. This sense of safety and validation is essential for the grieving individual to feel heard, understood, and supported during a time of profound sadness and vulnerability.

Empathy allows us to connect with the emotional experiences of others, to feel what they are feeling, and to understand their perspective on a deeper level. When we empathize with someone who is grieving, we validate their emotions and experiences, affirming that their feelings are normal and valid given the circumstances. This validation helps the grieving individual feel understood and accepted, which can provide immense comfort and reassurance during a time of grief.

Moreover, empathy enables us to offer genuine support and companionship to the grieving individual, allowing us to walk alongside them in their grief journey. By empathizing with their pain and sorrow, we show them that they are not alone in their grief and that we are there to offer comfort, understanding, and support whenever they need it.

Understanding is equally important in helping others navigate their grief. By taking the time to understand the unique experiences, needs, and coping mechanisms of the grieving individual, we can provide more effective support and assistance throughout the grieving process. Understanding allows us to tailor our support to better meet the needs of the grieving individual, whether it's through offering a listening ear, providing practical assistance, or simply being present with them in their pain.

In addition to providing comfort and validation, empathy and understanding also foster a deeper connection and trust between the supporter and the grieving individual. When someone feels truly understood and empathized with, they are more likely to open up and share their innermost thoughts and feelings. This deepens the bond between the supporter and the grieving individual, creating a sense of companionship and solidarity that can provide solace during the grieving process.

Furthermore, empathy and understanding help to normalize the grieving experience, showing the grieving individual that their emotions and reactions are a natural response to loss. This normalization can help alleviate feelings of isolation and self-judgment, allowing the grieving individual to accept and honor their emotions without shame or guilt.

Moreover, empathy and understanding empower the grieving individual to explore their grief in their own way and at their own pace. Rather than imposing our own expectations or timelines onto them, we honor their unique grieving process and provide the support they need to navigate it authentically. This autonomy and validation empower the grieving individual to take ownership of their grief journey and find their own path to healing and resilience.

Ultimately, empathy and understanding are not only acts of compassion and kindness, but they also serve as catalysts for healing and growth in the midst of grief. By approaching the grieving process with empathy and understanding, we create a space where the grieving individual feels seen, heard, and supported, paving the way for a journey of healing, acceptance, and ultimately, hope.

Chapter 6: Embracing Grief as Love

Embracing grief as love is a powerful concept that reframes the experience of grief as a continuation of the love we hold for the person we have lost. When we grieve deeply, it is a testament to the depth of our love and the impact that the person had on our lives. Instead of viewing grief as a negative or burdensome emotion, embracing it as love allows us to honor the connection we shared with our loved one and celebrate the memories, experiences, and moments of joy they brought into our lives.

By embracing grief as love, we acknowledge that the pain of loss is inseparable from the love we feel for the person who has passed away. Rather than trying to suppress or avoid our grief, we allow ourselves to fully experience and express it, recognizing that it is a natural and essential part of the healing process. In doing so, we honor the person we have lost and keep their memory alive through the love that continues to dwell within us.

Moreover, embracing grief as love enables us to find meaning and purpose in our grief journey. It inspires us to channel our love for the person who has passed away into acts of kindness, compassion, and service, both to ourselves and to others. By honoring our grief as a manifestation of love, we find healing, connection, and transformation in the midst of loss.

Embracing grief as love also allows us to find beauty and resilience in the midst of pain and loss. When we acknowledge that our grief is a reflection of the love we hold for our loved one, we recognize that love transcends physical presence and continues to exist beyond death. This realization can bring a sense of comfort and peace, knowing that the love we shared with our loved one is eternal and unchanging.

Furthermore, embracing grief as love encourages us to cherish and celebrate the memories, experiences, and moments of connection we shared with our loved one. Rather than dwelling solely on the pain of their absence, we focus on the love and joy they brought into our lives, honoring their legacy and the impact they had on us and others.

Moreover, embracing grief as love fosters a sense of interconnectedness and compassion within ourselves and with others who are grieving. When we recognize that grief is a universal human experience rooted in love, we can empathize with others who are navigating their own grief journey and offer them support, understanding, and solidarity.

In addition to fostering a deeper connection with our loved one and finding beauty in memories, embracing grief as love can also lead to personal growth and transformation. Through the process of grieving, we confront our deepest emotions, fears, and vulnerabilities, which can ultimately lead to profound self-discovery and inner healing.

When we embrace grief as love, we embark on a journey of self-exploration and reflection, seeking to understand the meaning and purpose of our loss in the context of our own lives. This journey often involves confronting difficult questions about life, death, and the nature of love, which can lead to greater clarity, wisdom, and insight.

Similarly, embracing grief as love can inspire us to live more intentionally and authentically, honoring the values and principles that were important to our loved one and embodying their legacy in our own lives. By channeling our grief into positive actions and meaningful pursuits, we honor the love we shared with our loved one and keep their memory alive through our words and deeds.

Furthermore, embracing grief as love can deepen our relationships with others and foster a greater sense of empathy, compassion, and connection within our communities. When we openly share our grief experiences and support one another through the grieving process, we create a culture of compassion and understanding that transcends boundaries and brings us closer together.

Ultimately, by embracing grief as love, we transform our pain and loss into a source of strength, resilience, and hope. We find solace in the knowledge that our love for our loved one will endure, and that their spirit lives on in the memories, values, and relationships we hold dear. In this way, grief becomes not just a journey of mourning, but a journey of love, growth, and transformation.

- Recognizing that grief is an expression of deep love

Recognizing that grief is an expression of deep love means understanding that every tear shed, every ache in your heart, and every longing for the one you've lost is a testament to the love you shared with them. It's acknowledging that the depth of your grief is a reflection of the depth of your love, and that your pain is a natural and profound expression of the bond you shared.

When you recognize grief as an expression of deep love, you validate the intensity of your emotions and the significance of your loss. You honor the love you felt for your loved one and the impact they had on your life. You understand that your grief is a natural and inevitable response to the profound sense of loss you're experiencing.

In addition to recognizing grief as an expression of deep love, it's important to acknowledge that the journey of grieving is unique to each individual. While the depth of your love may be reflected in the intensity of your grief, the way you experience and navigate that grief is entirely your own.

Embracing this understanding allows you to honor your personal grief journey and give yourself permission to feel and express your emotions authentically. You may find solace in rituals or activities that bring you closer to your loved one's memory, or you may seek comfort in sharing stories and memories with others who knew them. Whatever path you choose, remember that there is no right or wrong way to grieve, and it's okay to seek support and guidance along the way.

Furthermore, recognizing that grief is an expression of deep love can inspire you to find moments of beauty and connection amidst the pain. You may discover unexpected sources of comfort and joy in the memories you hold dear, or in the love and support of those around you. By embracing these moments, you honor the love you shared with your loved one and find strength in the bonds that endure beyond loss.

Additionally, recognizing grief as an expression of deep love invites you to cultivate a sense of gratitude for the time you shared with your loved one. While the pain of loss may feel overwhelming at times, reflecting on the love, laughter, and cherished moments you experienced together can bring a sense of warmth and appreciation to your heart.

By embracing gratitude amidst grief, you honor the love that continues to live on in your memories and the impact your loved one had on your life. You may find comfort in expressing gratitude for the lessons they taught you, the values they instilled in you, and the ways in which they enriched your life. This practice of gratitude can help shift your focus from the pain of loss to the beauty of the love that remains.

Moreover, embracing gratitude can inspire acts of kindness and generosity in honor of your loved one's memory. Whether it's volunteering your time, supporting a cause they were passionate about, or simply extending kindness to others in their name, these gestures serve as a tribute to the love you shared and a testament to the lasting impact they had on the world.

Also, recognizing grief as an expression of deep love invites you to embrace gratitude as a source of healing and connection. It reminds you that while grief may be a natural response to loss, love is a timeless and enduring force that transcends even the darkest of times.

Furthermore, recognizing grief as an expression of deep love allows you to embrace the bittersweet nature of the grieving process. While grief may bring intense pain and sorrow, it also serves as a testament to the depth of the connection you shared with your loved one. By acknowledging the complexity of grief, you honor the different nature of love itself – a web woven with both joy and sorrow, laughter and tears.

Embracing the bittersweet aspects of grief can lead to a deeper appreciation for the richness of life and the beauty of human connection. It reminds you that love is not confined to moments of happiness and fulfillment, but also encompasses the profound experience of loss and longing. Through this perspective, you may find moments of beauty and grace even in the midst of your pain, as you cherish the memories and experiences that continue to shape your journey.

Moreover, embracing the bittersweet nature of grief can inspire you to live more fully and authentically in honor of your loved one's memory. It encourages you to embrace each moment with gratitude and mindfulness, knowing that life is precious and fleeting. By living with intention and purpose, you carry forward the legacy of love that your loved one left behind, creating a ripple effect of positivity and kindness in the world.

In essence, recognizing grief as an expression of deep love invites you to embrace the full spectrum of human emotions and experiences. It encourages you to find beauty and meaning in the midst of pain, and to honor the love that continues to guide and inspire you on your journey. Through this perspective, you can find solace, strength, and resilience as you navigate the complexities of grief with grace and courage.

- Finding beauty and gratitude in the midst of sorrow

Finding beauty and gratitude in the midst of sorrow is a profound practice that allows us to shift our perspective and find moments of light amidst the darkness of grief. While the pain of loss may feel overwhelming, there are often glimpses of beauty and grace that can bring comfort and solace to our hearts.

One way to find beauty and gratitude in sorrow is to focus on the memories and experiences we shared with our loved one. Reflecting on the laughter, love, and cherished moments we experienced together can bring a sense of warmth and appreciation to our hearts, reminding us of the profound impact our loved one had on our lives.

Moreover, finding beauty and gratitude in sorrow involves embracing the lessons and blessings that emerge from our experiences of loss. While grief may bring intense pain and sadness, it also offers opportunities for growth, resilience, and connection. By acknowledging the ways in which grief has shaped us and enriched our lives, we can find gratitude for the strength and wisdom we have gained through our journey.

Additionally, finding beauty and gratitude in sorrow allows us to cultivate a sense of presence and mindfulness in the midst of our pain. By grounding ourselves in the present moment and savoring the simple pleasures of life, such as a beautiful sunset or a gentle breeze, we can find moments of peace and tranquility amidst the turmoil of grief.

Furthermore, finding beauty and gratitude in sorrow involves extending kindness and compassion to ourselves and others. By practicing self-care, reaching out for support, and offering comfort to those who are also grieving, we create a ripple effect of positivity and healing that can uplift and inspire us even in our darkest moments.

Additionally, finding beauty and gratitude in the midst of sorrow can inspire us to cultivate a deeper appreciation for the preciousness of life itself. When we experience loss, it serves as a poignant reminder of the impermanence of our existence and the importance of cherishing each moment we have with our loved ones.

Through the lens of grief, we may come to recognize the beauty in the ordinary – the warmth of a hug, the sound of laughter, the shared moments of joy and companionship. These simple yet profound experiences take on new significance as we realize their fleeting nature, prompting us to savor them more fully and express gratitude for their presence in our lives.

Moreover, finding beauty and gratitude in the midst of sorrow can inspire acts of kindness and generosity towards others who are also experiencing hardship or loss. By extending a helping hand, offering words of comfort, or simply being present for someone in need, we not only ease their burden but also cultivate a sense of connection and empathy that transcends our own grief.

Furthermore, finding beauty and gratitude in sorrow invites us to embrace the healing power of nature, art, and spirituality. Whether it's spending time in nature, immersing ourselves in creative expression, or finding solace in prayer or meditation, these practices can provide moments of respite and renewal amidst the pain of grief.

Let me share a story with you that beautifully illustrates finding beauty and gratitude in the midst of sorrow is the experience of a woman named Andrea, who lost her twin sister unexpectedly to cancer. Despite the overwhelming grief and devastation she felt, Andrea made a conscious effort to find moments of beauty and gratitude in the midst of her sorrow.

Andrea found solace in nature, taking long walks in the park near her home and immersing herself in the beauty of the natural world. She found comfort in the gentle rustle of the leaves, the soothing sound of flowing water, and the vibrant colors of the flowers in bloom. In these moments, Andrea felt a sense of peace and connection to something greater than herself, allowing her to find beauty amidst the pain of her loss.

Moreover, Andrea found gratitude in the memories she shared with her sister and the love they had for each other. She created a gratitude journal where she wrote down moments of joy, laughter, and love they had experienced together. Through this practice, Andrea found healing in the act of remembering and expressing gratitude for the time they had shared, rather than dwelling on the pain of her sister's absence.

Additionally, Andrea found beauty and gratitude in the support of her friends and family, who rallied around her with love and compassion during her darkest days. Their kindness, empathy, and unwavering presence reminded Andrea that she was not alone in her grief and gave her strength to carry on.

Through her journey of finding beauty and gratitude in the midst of sorrow, Andrea discovered a newfound sense of resilience, hope, and purpose. While the pain of her loss would always be a part of her, she learned to embrace the beauty of life and cherish each moment with gratitude and appreciation. In doing so, Andrea found healing, strength, and a renewed sense of connection to the world around her.

- Honoring your loved one's legacy through acts of kindness and compassion

Honoring your loved one's legacy through acts of kindness and compassion is a deeply meaningful way to keep their memory alive and continue the love they shared with the world. When we lose someone dear to us, finding ways to honor their legacy can bring comfort and purpose amidst the pain of grief.

One powerful way to honor your loved one's legacy is through acts of kindness and compassion . It can serve as a source of inspiration and empowerment for yourself and others. When you actively seek out opportunities to make a positive impact in the world, you not only honor the memory of your loved one but also reaffirm your own ability to effect change and make a difference.

Engaging in acts of kindness and compassion can also provide a sense of connection to your loved one, as you channel their spirit and values into tangible actions that uplift and support others. Whether it's through volunteering, charitable giving, or simply offering a kind word or gesture to someone in need, each act of kindness becomes a tribute to the love and generosity they embodied.

Moreover, honoring your loved one's legacy through acts of kindness and compassion can foster a sense of healing and renewal in the midst of grief. By focusing on the positive impact you can make in the world, you shift your perspective from loss and sorrow to hope and possibility. In doing so, you find solace and purpose in knowing that your loved one's legacy lives on through your actions.

Additionally, engaging in acts of kindness and compassion can create a ripple effect of positivity that extends far beyond your own circle of influence. Your actions have the power to inspire others to do the same, creating a chain reaction of kindness and generosity that spreads throughout your community and beyond. In this way, you become a living testament to the enduring impact of your loved one's legacy.

In essence, honoring your loved one's legacy through acts of kindness and compassion is a powerful and transformative practice that celebrates their life, honors their memory, and brings healing and hope to yourself and others. By embracing the opportunity to make a positive difference in the world, you keep their spirit alive and create a legacy of love and goodness that endures long after they are gone.

Furthermore, honoring your loved one's legacy through acts of kindness and compassion can serve as a bridge between the past and the future, creating a sense of continuity and connection across generations. By sharing stories, memories, and lessons learned from your loved one with younger family members or community members, you pass on their values, beliefs, and traditions, ensuring that their legacy lives on for generations to come.

Engaging in acts of kindness and compassion can also provide a sense of purpose and fulfillment in the midst of grief, as you find meaning in making a positive difference in the lives of others. Whether it's volunteering at a local charity, organizing a fundraiser in honor of your loved one, or simply lending a helping hand to someone in need, each act becomes a tribute to their memory and a testament to the love they shared.

Moreover, honoring your loved one's legacy through acts of kindness and compassion can serve as a form of self-care and healing for yourself. By focusing your energy on giving back and making a positive impact, you shift the focus from your own pain and sorrow to the needs of others, finding solace and comfort in knowing that you are making a difference in the world.

Additionally, engaging in acts of kindness and compassion can help you find a sense of closure and acceptance in your grief journey. By actively honoring your loved one's memory and continuing their legacy of love and kindness, you create a sense of continuity and connection that transcends their physical absence, allowing their spirit to live on in the hearts and minds of those they touched.

Let's consider this story which beautifully illustrates the concept of honoring a loved one's legacy through acts of kindness and compassion is the journey of Maria, whose father passed away after a long battle with illness.

Maria's father was a pillar of strength and kindness in their community, known for his selfless acts of generosity and unwavering compassion towards others. Inspired by his example, Maria made a commitment to honor his memory by continuing his legacy of kindness and compassion.

Shortly after her father's passing, Maria decided to volunteer at a local soup kitchen, where she could directly impact the lives of those in need, just as her father had done. She spent countless hours serving meals, lending a listening ear, and offering words of encouragement to those who were struggling.

Through her volunteer work, Maria not only found solace and healing in the act of giving back but also discovered a newfound sense of purpose and fulfillment in her own life. Each act of kindness became a tribute to her father's memory, a way to honor the love and generosity he had shown to others throughout his life.

As Maria continued to engage in acts of kindness and compassion, she found herself inspired to do even more to carry forward her father's legacy. She organized a charity fundraiser in his honor, raising funds to support families affected by the same illness that had taken her father's life. She also initiated a community service project, inviting others to join her in cleaning up local parks and beautifying public spaces in memory of her father.

Through these meaningful actions, Maria not only kept her father's memory alive but also inspired others to join her in honoring his legacy. Together, they created a ripple effect of kindness and compassion that touched the lives of countless individuals in their community, spreading love and goodwill in the face of grief and loss.

In essence, Maria's story serves as a powerful reminder of the transformative power of honoring a loved one's legacy through acts of kindness and compassion. By channeling her grief into positive action, she not only found healing and purpose in her own life but also created a lasting tribute to the love and generosity of her father, ensuring that his spirit would live on in the hearts and minds of those he touched.

Chapter 7: The Healing Power of Grief

The healing power of grief is a profound and often misunderstood aspect of the human experience. While grief is commonly associated with pain and sorrow, it also has the capacity to be a transformative and healing force in our lives.

One of the most powerful aspects of grief is its ability to allow us to process and release the intense emotions associated with loss. By allowing ourselves to fully experience and express our grief, we create space for healing to occur. This process of mourning enables us to gradually come to terms with the reality of our loss and begin to integrate it into our lives in a way that feels meaningful and manageable.

Moreover, grief has the power to deepen our connections with others and foster a sense of community and support. In times of loss, we often turn to our loved ones for comfort and companionship, and in doing so, we strengthen our bonds with one another. Sharing our grief with others can also help to alleviate feelings of isolation and loneliness, reminding us that we are not alone in our pain.

Additionally, grief has the capacity to inspire personal growth and transformation. Through the process of grieving, we are forced to confront our own mortality and reevaluate our priorities and values. This introspection can lead to profound insights and shifts in perspective, ultimately guiding us towards a greater sense of meaning and purpose in our lives.

Furthermore, grief can serve as a catalyst for positive change and action. In the face of loss, many individuals find themselves motivated to honor their loved one's memory by making a positive impact in the world. Whether through acts of kindness and compassion, charitable endeavors, or advocacy work, these actions can not only bring healing to the individual but also create a lasting legacy of love and generosity.

Similarly , the healing power of grief lies in its ability to deepen our understanding of ourselves and our emotions. Through the process of grieving, we become more attuned to our innermost thoughts and feelings, allowing us to develop greater emotional intelligence and self-awareness. As we navigate the ups and downs of grief, we learn to recognize and acknowledge our own needs, boundaries, and strengths, empowering us to cultivate a deeper sense of self-compassion and resilience.

Additionally, grief has the capacity to foster spiritual growth and exploration. For many people, the experience of loss prompts profound questions about the nature of life, death, and existence, leading to a search for deeper meaning and purpose. Through practices such as meditation, prayer, or contemplation, individuals may find solace and insight in connecting with their spirituality and exploring the mysteries of the universe.

Moreover, the healing power of grief extends beyond the individual to encompass broader societal and cultural shifts. As communities come together to mourn and support one another in times of loss, they often experience a renewed sense of solidarity and compassion. This collective grief can spark conversations about important issues such as mental health, end-of-life care, and social justice, paving the way for positive change and progress in our society.

Also, the healing power of grief can manifest in unexpected ways through creative expression. Many individuals find solace and catharsis in artistic endeavors such as writing, painting, music, or dance during times of grief. Engaging in these creative outlets allows for the expression of complex emotions that may be difficult to articulate verbally. Through the process of creating art, individuals can externalize their innermost thoughts and feelings, gaining a sense of release and clarity in the process.

Furthermore , creative expression can serve as a bridge between the conscious and unconscious mind, unlocking deeper layers of insight and understanding. By tapping into the subconscious through artistic expression, individuals may uncover hidden emotions, memories, and truths about themselves and their relationship with the deceased. This process of self-discovery can be profoundly healing, offering new perspectives and pathways for growth.

Additionally, sharing creative work with others can create connections and foster empathy and understanding. Art has the power to transcend language and cultural barriers, speaking directly to the heart and soul of the viewer or listener. Through sharing their creative expressions with others, individuals who are grieving can find validation, support, and a sense of belonging in a community of fellow travelers on the journey of loss and healing.

In essence, the healing power of grief is not limited to traditional forms of expression or coping mechanisms. Through the transformative potential of creativity, individuals can find solace, meaning, and connection in the midst of their grief journey.

- Understanding that healing from grief is not about getting over it, but about learning to live with it

Understanding that healing from grief is not about getting over it, but about learning to live with it is a fundamental shift in perspective that acknowledges the ongoing nature of the grieving process. While society often expects individuals to "move on" from their grief within a certain timeframe, the reality is that grief does not have an expiration date. Instead, it becomes integrated into the fabric of our lives, shaping our thoughts, feelings, and actions in profound ways.

This understanding allows individuals to embrace the ebb and flow of grief with greater acceptance and compassion. Rather than viewing grief as something to be overcome or conquered, they recognize it as a natural and inevitable part of the human experience. By reframing their relationship with grief in this way, individuals can release the pressure to "get back to normal" and instead focus on finding a new normal that accommodates the presence of their loss.

Moreover, learning to live with grief involves cultivating resilience and adaptability in the face of life's challenges and changes. It requires developing coping strategies and self-care practices that support emotional well-being and promote healing. This may include seeking support from loved ones, engaging in therapy or counseling, practicing mindfulness and relaxation techniques, or participating in support groups or grief rituals.

Furthermore, learning to live with grief invites individuals to honor the memory of their loved one in meaningful ways. This may involve creating rituals or traditions that commemorate special occasions or milestones, sharing stories and memories with others, or finding ways to carry forward their loved one's values and legacy through acts of kindness and compassion.

Furthermore, understanding that healing from grief is a lifelong journey encourages individuals to practice patience and self-compassion as they navigate the ups and downs of grief. It reminds them that there is no "right" or "wrong" way to grieve and that everyone's journey is unique. By giving themselves permission to experience grief in their own time and in their own way, individuals can cultivate greater acceptance and understanding of their emotions and experiences.

Additionally, learning to live with grief invites individuals to embrace the lessons and insights that come from their journey of loss. Through the process of grieving, individuals may discover newfound strengths, resilience, and wisdom that can enrich their lives and deepen their connections with others. By honoring the transformative potential of grief, individuals can find meaning and purpose in their experiences, even amidst the pain and sorrow.

Moreover, understanding that healing from grief is about learning to live with it acknowledges the ongoing impact that loss can have on individuals and their relationships. It encourages open and honest communication with loved ones about their needs, boundaries, and feelings, fostering deeper connections and mutual support. By creating a supportive environment where grief is acknowledged and validated, individuals can find comfort and solace in the presence of others who understand and empathize with their experiences.

Furthermore, understanding that healing from grief is not about getting over it, but about learning to live with it, emphasizes the importance of finding balance in life. When individuals are grieving, it can be easy to become consumed by their emotions and the process of mourning. However, it's essential to also find moments of respite, joy, and connection amidst the grief.

Finding balance may involve engaging in activities that bring comfort and solace, such as spending time in nature, practicing creative expression, or immersing oneself in hobbies and interests. It may also involve seeking out moments of laughter and connection with loved ones, even amidst the pain of loss. By allowing space for both grief and moments of joy, individuals can cultivate a sense of equilibrium and resilience in their lives.

Additionally, understanding that healing from grief is a journey of learning to live with it encourages individuals to practice self-compassion and forgiveness. Grief can often bring up feelings of guilt, regret, or self-blame, as individuals grapple with questions of what could have been done differently or whether they could have prevented the loss. By offering themselves kindness and understanding, individuals can release themselves from the burden of these negative emotions and embrace a sense of acceptance and peace.

Moreover, finding meaning and purpose in the midst of grief can be a powerful source of healing. Whether it's through finding ways to honor the memory of a loved one, making positive changes in the world, or deepening connections with others, individuals can find a sense of fulfillment and significance amidst the pain of loss. By aligning their actions with their values and beliefs, individuals can create a legacy of love and compassion that honors their loved one's memory and brings meaning to their own lives.

- Embracing the pain and transforming it into strength and resilience

Embracing the pain of grief and transforming it into strength and resilience is a powerful and transformative process that allows individuals to reclaim their sense of agency and empowerment in the face of loss. Rather than allowing grief to overwhelm or define them, individuals can harness its energy to fuel their journey towards healing and growth.

One way to embrace the pain of grief is to allow oneself to fully experience and express the range of emotions that come with it. This may involve giving oneself permission to cry, scream, or rage against the injustice of loss. By acknowledging and honoring the depth of one's pain, individuals can begin to release its hold on them and open themselves up to the possibility of healing.

Moreover, embracing the pain of grief involves recognizing the lessons and insights that can be gained from the experience of loss. Grief has the power to teach us about the fragility of life, the importance of love and connection, and the resilience of the human spirit. By embracing these lessons, individuals can cultivate a greater sense of wisdom, compassion, and gratitude in their lives.

In addition , transforming the pain of grief into strength and resilience requires a commitment to self-care and self-compassion. This may involve seeking out support from loved ones, engaging in therapeutic practices such as journaling or meditation, or accessing professional help when needed. By prioritizing their own well-being, individuals can build the inner resources and resilience needed to navigate the challenges of grief with grace and courage.

Furthermore, embracing the pain of grief and transforming it into strength and resilience involves acknowledging the interconnectedness of joy and sorrow in the human experience. Just as grief can bring intense pain and sorrow, it can also deepen our capacity for empathy, compassion, and connection with others who are suffering. By recognizing the shared humanity in our experiences of loss, individuals can find solace and solidarity in knowing that they are not alone in their grief.

Not only that, embracing the pain of grief requires a willingness to confront the difficult truths and uncertainties of life. Loss can shatter our illusions of control and security, forcing us to confront the impermanence of existence and the inevitability of change. By embracing the reality of impermanence and learning to live with a sense of openness and acceptance, individuals can cultivate greater resilience and adaptability in the face of life's challenges.

Also , embracing the pain of grief requires a willingness to embrace vulnerability and allow oneself to be supported by others. It can be tempting to withdraw or isolate oneself in times of grief, but true healing often comes from connecting with others and allowing oneself to be seen and held in their love and compassion. By reaching out for support and allowing others to walk alongside us on our journey of grief, we not only find strength in community but also deepen our capacity for empathy and connection.

On top of that, embracing the pain of grief and transforming it into strength and resilience involves recognizing the interconnectedness of all living beings and the universal experience of loss. While grief may feel isolating and deeply personal, it is a shared human experience that transcends cultural, religious, and geographical boundaries. By acknowledging our common humanity and the universality of grief, we can find solace in knowing that we are not alone in our struggles.

Similarly , embracing the pain of grief requires a willingness to confront our own mortality and existential questions about the nature of life and death. While these inquiries may be unsettling, they also offer an opportunity for deeper reflection and spiritual exploration. By grappling with these existential truths, we can gain a deeper appreciation for the preciousness of life and the interconnectedness of all beings.

- Finding hope and courage in the face of profound loss

Finding hope and courage in the face of profound loss is a testament to the resilience of the human spirit and the power of the human heart to endure even the darkest of times. While grief may feel all-encompassing and insurmountable, there is a spark of hope that flickers within us, guiding us through the darkness and urging us to keep moving forward.

One way to find hope and courage in the face of loss is to draw strength from the memories and legacies of our loved ones. Even though they may no longer be physically present, their spirit lives on in the hearts and minds of those they touched. By cherishing the memories we shared with them and honoring their legacy through our actions, we can find solace and inspiration in their enduring presence.

Moreover, finding hope and courage in the face of loss involves recognizing the resilience and adaptability of the human spirit. While grief may initially feel overwhelming and all-consuming, it is also a testament to our capacity to heal and grow. By allowing ourselves to feel and process our emotions, we create space for healing and transformation to occur, paving the way for a brighter future.

Additionally, finding hope and courage in the face of loss requires a willingness to embrace the support and compassion of others. While grief can feel isolating, it is important to remember that we are not alone in our struggles. By reaching out for support from loved ones, friends, or support groups, we can find comfort and strength in the connections we share with others who understand and empathize with our experiences.

Similarly , finding hope and courage in the face of loss requires a willingness to embrace uncertainty and trust in the journey of healing. While grief may feel overwhelming and uncertain, there is a resilience within us that allows us to navigate the unknown with courage and grace. By surrendering to the process of grief and allowing ourselves to be vulnerable, we open ourselves up to the possibility of growth and transformation.

In addition , finding hope and courage in the face of profound loss involves recognizing the transformative potential of our grief journey. While grief may initially feel like an overwhelming and debilitating force, it also holds the possibility for profound personal growth and spiritual evolution. By embracing our grief as a teacher and guide, we can uncover hidden strengths, deepen our empathy and compassion, and cultivate a greater appreciation for the preciousness of life.

On top of that, finding hope and courage in the face of loss requires a commitment to living authentically and with intention. Grief has a way of stripping away the trivialities and distractions of life, allowing us to focus on what truly matters most. By embracing this newfound clarity and authenticity, we can align our actions with our values and aspirations, finding purpose and meaning even in the midst of pain and uncertainty.

Additionally, finding hope and courage in the face of loss involves recognizing the power of love to transcend even the deepest of sorrows. Love is what connects us to our loved ones, even after they have passed, and it is what gives us the strength to carry on in their absence. By nurturing the love that we shared with our loved ones and extending that love to ourselves and others, we can find solace and comfort in the midst of grief.

Epilogue: A Love Letter to Grief

Writing a love letter to grief is an intimate and personal act that involves expressing emotions, thoughts, and experiences related to the process of grieving. It provides individuals with a platform to communicate directly with their grief, acknowledging its presence and impact on their lives.

In this form of self-expression, individuals have the opportunity to delve deep into their feelings and memories associated with their loss. By putting pen to paper, they can articulate the complexities of their grief journey, from the initial shock and disbelief to the eventual acceptance and healing. Through the act of writing, they can navigate through the various stages of grief, allowing themselves to experience and process each emotion fully.

Moreover, writing a love letter to grief allows individuals to find meaning and purpose in their loss. They can reflect on the relationship they shared with the deceased, recounting cherished memories and expressing gratitude for the time they had together. This act of remembrance can be both comforting and cathartic, providing a sense of connection to the person they have lost and reaffirming the love that continues to endure beyond death.

Additionally, writing a love letter to grief fosters a sense of self-awareness and introspection. It encourages individuals to explore their innermost thoughts and feelings, gaining insight into their own coping mechanisms and resilience. By confronting their grief head-on, they can begin to make sense of their emotions and find a sense of peace amidst the turmoil of loss.

Furthermore, writing a love letter to grief can be a transformative experience, facilitating personal growth and healing. It allows individuals to release pent-up emotions and find closure, paving the way for acceptance and reconciliation. Through this process of self-expression, they can embrace their grief as a natural and integral part of the human experience, honoring the memory of their loved one while also embracing the possibility of a new chapter in their lives.

Permit me to share with you some letters penned by those grieving to their loved ones as a part of healing on their own part.

My Dearest Grief,

As you envelop me in your somber embrace, I cannot help but acknowledge the profound impact you have had on my life since the departure of my beloved daughter . Your presence, though initially overwhelming, has become a companion of sorts, guiding me through the labyrinth of loss and longing.

Your arrival was met with resistance, a natural response to the void left by her absence. Each day without my baby girl felt like a dagger to the heart, a reminder of the

moments we will never share again. Your presence served as a constant reminder of what once was and what will never be again.

Yet, as time has passed, I have come to see you in a different light. You are not merely a harbinger of sorrow, but a catalyst for growth and understanding. Through your presence, I have learned to confront the depths of my pain, to sift through the fragments of memories with a newfound clarity.

In your shadow, I have discovered the beauty of impermanence, the fleeting nature of life and love. You have taught me to cherish each moment with a reverence that transcends time, to find solace in the bittersweet dance of joy and sorrow that defines the human experience.

And so, dear Grief, I write to you not with bitterness or resentment, but with a heart filled with gratitude. You have been my steadfast companion on this journey of healing, guiding me through the darkest of nights towards the dawn of a new day. Through your presence, I have found strength I never knew I possessed, resilience in the face of adversity.

Though your presence may linger, I know that you are not here to stay. Like the changing seasons, you will eventually recede, leaving behind the gentle whisper of acceptance and peace. And when that time comes, I will bid you farewell with a heart full of love and gratitude, knowing that you have been a faithful teacher and friend.

With deepest gratitude,

Annabella

My Dearest Cady ,

As I sit here, penning these words to you, I am overwhelmed by the weight of your absence and the depths of the grief I am experiencing in your absence. It feels as though a piece of my soul has been torn away, leaving behind an emptiness that cannot be filled.

Each day without you is a struggle, a relentless battle against the tide of sorrow that threatens to engulf me. Your departure has left a void in my life that cannot be filled, a silence that echoes in the chambers of my heart.

I find myself yearning for your presence, longing for the sound of your laughter and the warmth of your embrace. The memories of our time together are both a source of comfort and a source of pain. In the depths of my grief, I am reminded of the depth of our love, a love that transcends the boundaries of time and space. Though you may no longer be by my side, your spirit lives on in the memories we shared and the love that continues to bind us together.

But even as I grapple with the pain of your absence, I am filled with gratitude for the time we had together. You brought so much joy and light into my life, and for that, I will be forever grateful. Though you may no longer be with me in body, your presence continues to guide me, to inspire me, to fill me with hope for the future.

And so, my dearest Cady, I write to you with a heart heavy with grief but also overflowing with love. Though you may no longer be here with me, your spirit will always live on in my heart, a beacon of light in the darkness, a source of strength and solace in my time of need.

With all my love,

Riley

My Dearest Grief,

As the bearer of this message, I entrust you with conveying my deepest sentiments to my dear friend —Lucius — who has departed from this earthly realm. Though their physical presence may be absent, their spirit lingers in the memories we shared and the love that continues to permeate my existence.

Grief, you have been a constant companion on this journey of loss, a faithful messenger carrying the weight of my sorrow. Yet, amidst the pain and longing, I want you to know that I am okay, and I will also appreciate it if you will tell Lucius that , despite the ache in my heart and the tears that stain my cheeks, I am okay.

For in the depths of my grief, I have found a profound sense of peace and acceptance. Though I will always cherish the memories we created together, I have come to understand that his departure was not an end, but a transformation. He have become a part of me, woven into the fabric of my being, guiding me with your love and wisdom.

And so, as you carry this message to my Lucius, I ask that you reassure him of my well-being. Let him know that I am okay, that I am finding my way through the darkness with courage and grace. And though I may stumble and falter along the way, I am held by the love that we shared and his memories that sustain me.

With deepest gratitude,

Reecelius

Just like you can see above , writing a love letter to grief is a deeply personal and therapeutic practice that can offer comfort, insight, and healing to those navigating the turbulent waters of loss. It provides a safe space for individuals to express themselves fully, allowing them to find solace and meaning in the midst of their sorrow.

- A heartfelt message of gratitude for the transformative power of grief

In expressing heartfelt gratitude for the transformative power of grief, you acknowledge the profound impact it has had on your life's journey. At first glance, grief may appear as an unwelcome intruder, disrupting the fabric of your existence and leaving behind a trail of pain and sorrow. Yet, as you delve deeper into its depths, you begin to recognize the hidden potential for growth, resilience, and self-discovery that lies within.

Through the tumultuous journey of grieving, you confront your deepest fears, vulnerabilities, and insecurities. You are forced to navigate the turbulent waters of loss, grappling with the harsh realities of impermanence and the fragility of life itself. In this crucible of grief, you unearth reservoirs of strength and courage you never knew existed, drawing upon them to navigate the darkest of nights.

In addition to the transformative power of grief, it's important to acknowledge the role it plays in shaping our relationships and perspectives. Grief has a way of illuminating the bonds that connect us to others, deepening our appreciation for the love and support that surrounds us. Through the lens of loss, we often gain a newfound clarity about the value of our relationships and the importance of cherishing every moment we have with those we hold dear.

Moreover, grief can serve as a catalyst for personal growth and spiritual awakening. As we navigate the rocky terrain of grief, we are compelled to confront our deepest fears and confront the impermanence of life. This process of introspection and self-examination can lead to profound insights and transformations, ultimately guiding us towards a more authentic and purposeful way of living.

Furthermore, grief has the power to inspire acts of kindness and compassion towards others who are also experiencing loss. In the midst of our own pain and sorrow, we often find solace in reaching out to others, offering a listening ear, a comforting embrace, or a simple gesture of support. In this way, grief becomes a force for good, fostering a sense of unity and solidarity within our communities.

Ultimately, expressing gratitude for the transformative power of grief is a testament to the resilience of the human spirit and the capacity of the heart to heal and grow. It is a recognition of the profound impact that loss can have on our lives, and a celebration of the strength and courage that emerges from the depths of sorrow. And as we navigate the ever-changing landscape of grief, we are reminded of the enduring power of love to guide us through even the darkest of times.

- Embracing grief as a part of life's journey, filled with love and compassion

Embracing grief as a part of life's journey is a profound acknowledgment of the inherent beauty and complexity of the human experience. It is a recognition that grief, far from being a sign of weakness or failure, is a natural and inevitable aspect of our existence – a testament to the depth of our capacity to love and connect with others.

When we embrace grief as a part of life's journey, we open ourselves up to a deeper understanding of the human condition. We recognize that loss is an integral part of the human experience, and that our ability to navigate through grief is a testament to our resilience and strength. In this way, grief becomes a teacher, guiding us towards a deeper appreciation for the fragility and preciousness of life.

Moreover, embracing grief allows us to cultivate a sense of compassion and empathy towards ourselves and others. When we acknowledge our own pain and sorrow, we create space for healing and growth, allowing ourselves to process our emotions in a healthy and constructive way. And when we extend that same compassion to others who are experiencing grief, we foster a sense of connection and solidarity that transcends individual suffering.

In addition to embracing grief as a natural part of life's journey, it's important to recognize the transformative power it holds. Grief has the potential to catalyze profound personal growth and inner healing, leading to a deeper understanding of ourselves and our place in the world.

Also, when we embrace grief with an open heart and a spirit of acceptance, we create space for transformation to occur. We allow ourselves to lean into the discomfort of loss, to sit with the pain and sadness, and to explore the depths of our emotions without judgment or resistance. In this process, we often uncover hidden reserves of strength, resilience, and wisdom that we never knew we possessed.

Similarly , embracing grief opens the door to profound spiritual insights and awakening. As we navigate the tumultuous waters of loss, we are confronted with the ultimate questions of existence – the nature of life, death, and the meaning of our own existence. In this quest for understanding, we may find solace in spiritual practices, rituals, or beliefs that offer comfort and guidance along the journey.

On top of that , embracing grief fosters a sense of connection and empathy towards others who are also grappling with loss. Through our own experiences of pain and sorrow, we become more attuned to the suffering of those around us, and more willing to extend a hand of compassion and support. In this way, grief becomes a catalyst for building stronger, more compassionate communities that are grounded in mutual understanding and solidarity.

Ultimately, embracing grief as a part of life's journey is an invitation to surrender to the ebb and flow of human experience – to embrace the fullness of life, with all its joys and sorrows, triumphs and tribulations. It is a testament to the resilience of the human spirit, and a celebration of the profound capacity of the heart to heal and grow, even in the face of the greatest adversity.

- Encouragement to continue moving forward with courage and resilience

In times of grief and loss, it's natural to feel overwhelmed and uncertain about the future. However, it's important to remember that within you lies a wellspring of courage and resilience, waiting to be tapped into. Despite the darkness that may surround you, there is always a glimmer of light – a beacon of hope that guides you forward on your journey.

You are stronger than you realize, capable of weathering even the most tempestuous storms.

Each step you take forward, no matter how small, is a testament to your inner strength and determination. Even in the face of adversity, you have the power to rise above your circumstances and chart a course towards healing and renewal.

Take heart in the knowledge that grief is not a sign of weakness, but rather a testament to the depth of your capacity to love and connect with others. It is through the process of grieving that we learn to honor the memories of our loved ones while also embracing the present moment with gratitude and resilience.

So, I encourage you to continue moving forward with courage and resilience, knowing that you are not alone on this journey. Reach out to friends, family, or support networks for guidance and companionship. Lean into your emotions, allowing yourself to feel them fully without judgment or resistance. And above all, trust in your own inner strength and resilience to carry you through even the darkest of times.

Remember, grief is not the end of your story, but rather a chapter in the larger tapestry of your life. With each passing day, you grow stronger, wiser, and more resilient – a testament to the indomitable spirit that resides within you. So, take heart, dear friend, and continue moving forward with courage and resilience, knowing that brighter days lie ahead.

Conclusion

In conclusion, embracing grief as a pathway to healing is a courageous and transformative journey that offers profound lessons and insights to those who dare to embark upon it. Throughout this journey, we learn that grief is not a sign of weakness, but rather a testament to the depth of our capacity to love and connect with others. It teaches us to honor the memories of our loved ones while also embracing the present moment with gratitude and resilience.

As we navigate the ups and downs of grief with courage and resilience, we discover hidden reservoirs of strength, wisdom, and compassion within ourselves. We learn to lean into our emotions, allowing ourselves to feel them fully without judgment or resistance. And through the process of grieving, we find healing and renewal, as we embrace the fullness of life with all its joys and sorrows.

I encourage readers to embrace their grief as a source of love and growth, trusting in their own inner strength and resilience to guide them through even the darkest of times. Know that you are not alone on this journey – there is hope and support available to you, from friends, family, and support networks who understand the pain of loss and are ready to offer a listening ear or a comforting embrace.

So, take heart, dear reader, and know that brighter days lie ahead. Embrace your grief as a pathway to healing, knowing that it is through the depths of sorrow that we discover the true meaning of love and the resilience of the human spirit. May you find comfort, solace, and peace on your own grief journey, knowing that you are surrounded by love and supported by those who care for you.